COGAT® TEST PREP • LEVEL 7

Revised Edition With Updated Introduction & 300 Questions

Gateway Gifted Resources™
www.GatewayGifted.com

PLEASE LEAVE US
A REVIEW!

Thank you for selecting this book. We are a family-owned publishing company - a consortium of educators, test designers, book designers, parents, and kid-testers.

We would be thrilled if you left us a quick review on the website where you purchased this book!

The Gateway Gifted Resources™ Team
www.GatewayGifted.com

TABLE OF CONTENTS

INTRODUCTION

- Introduction (About The COGAT® & About This Book) 4
- Test-Taking Tips 5
- The Gifted Detective Agency 5
- Question Examples & Explanations 6

WORKBOOK

- Skill Builders 10
- Picture Analogies 16
- Figure Analogies 20
- Picture Classification 22
- Figure Classification 26
- Can You Find It? (Sentence Completion) 28
- Paper Folding Puzzles 32
- Number Series (Abacus Activity) 38
- Number Puzzles (Train Activity) 41
- Number Analogies 44

PRACTICE QUESTION SET

- Practice Question Set Instructions 49
- Verbal Section 50
- Quantitative Section 64
- Non-Verbal Section 78

ANSWER KEYS & DIRECTIONS FOR PRACTICE QUESTION SET

- Answer Key for Workbook 90
- Directions and Answer Key for Practice Question Set 91

ADDITIONAL BOOKS AND FREE E-BOOK INFORMATION 96

CHILD CERTIFICATE 96

ABOUT THE COGAT® LEVEL 7: The COGAT® (Cognitive Abilities Test®) Level 7 is given to children in first grade. As the name suggests, it assesses your child's cognitive skills. The test is divided into 3 "batteries." Each of the batteries has 3 question types. The Verbal Battery's question types are Picture Analogies, Picture Classification, and Sentence Completion. The Non-Verbal Battery's question types are Figure Analogies, Figure Classification, and Paper Folding. The Quantitative Battery's question types are Number Analogies, Number Puzzles, and Number Series. Each question type has 16 questions, except for Paper Folding and Number Puzzles, which have 12 questions each. The test has 136 questions total. The test, about two to three hours in length, is administered in different testing sessions. Children are not expected to complete 136 questions in one session. **See p.6-9 for more on these question types.**

ABOUT COGAT® TESTING PROCEDURES: These vary by school. Tests may be given individually or in a group. These tests may be used as the single factor for admission to gifted programs, or they may be used in combination with IQ tests or as part of a student "portfolio." They are used by some schools together with tests like Iowa Assessments™ to measure academic achievement. Check with your testing site to determine its specific testing procedures.

ABOUT THIS BOOK: This book introduces cognitive skill-building exercises to early elementary-age children through child-friendly subjects. The format is designed to help prepare children taking standardized multiple-choice gifted and talented assessment tests like the COGAT®. This book has five parts.

1. Introduction (p.4-9): About the COGAT® and about this book (p.4); Test Taking Tips (p.5), The Gifted Detective Agency (p.5), and Question Examples & Explanations (p.6-9).

2. Workbook (p.10-48): Pages 10-15 are designed as skill-building activities, while pages 16-48 are designed similarly to content tested in the COGAT®'s nine test question types. The Workbook exercises are meant to be done together with no time limit. **Before doing the Workbook with your child, read the Question Examples & Explanations (p.6-9).**

3. Practice Question Set (p.50-89): The Practice Question Set helps children develop critical thinking and test-taking skills. A "score" (a percentile rank) cannot be obtained from this. (See below for more on gifted test scoring.) It provides an introduction to standardized test-taking in a relaxed manner (parents may provide guidance if needed). It is an opportunity for children to practice focusing on a group of questions for a longer time period (something to which some children are not accustomed). It is also a way for parents to identify points of strength/ weakness in COGAT® question types. It is divided into three sections to mirror the three COGAT® batteries: Verbal, Quantitative, and Non-Verbal.

4. Directions and Answer Keys (p.90-95): These pages contain answer keys for both the Workbook and the Practice Question Set. They also include the directions to read to your child for the Practice Question Set. (To mimic actual tests, the directions are separate from the child's pages in the Practice Question Set.)

5. Afterword (p.96): Information on additional books, free eBook of practice questions, and your child's certificate

QUESTION NOTE: Because each child has different cognitive abilities, the questions in this book are at varied skill levels. The exercises may or may not require a great deal of parental guidance to complete, depending on your child's abilities and familiarity with this multiple choice question format. Most sections of the Workbook begin with a relatively easy question. We suggest always completing at least the first question together, ensuring your child is not confused about what the question asks or with the directions.

"BUBBLES" NOTE: Your child will most likely have to fill in "bubbles" (the circles) to indicate answer choices. (Check with your testing site regarding its "bubble" use.) Show your child how to fill in the bubble to indicate his/her answer choice using a pencil. If your child needs to change his/her answer, (s)he should erase the original mark and fill in the new choice.

SCORING NOTE: Check with your school/program for its specific scoring and admissions requirements. Here is a general summary of the scoring process. First, your child's raw score is established. This is the number of questions correctly answered. Points are not deducted for questions answered incorrectly. Next, this score is compared to other test-takers of his/her same age group (and, for the COGAT®, the same grade level) using various indices to then calculate your child's stanine (a score from one to nine) and percentile rank. If your child achieved the percentile rank of 98%, then (s)he scored as well as or better than 98% of test-takers. In general, gifted programs accept scores of *at least* 98% or *higher*. Please note that a percentile rank "score" cannot be obtained from our practice material. This material has not been given to a large enough sample of test-takers to develop any kind of base score necessary for percentile rank calculations.

TEST TAKING TIPS
• Have your child practice listening carefully. Paying attention is important, because test questions are not repeated.
• In the Workbook section, go through the exercises together by talking about them: what the exercise is asking the child to do and what makes the answer choices correct/incorrect. This will not only familiarize your child with working through exercises, it will also help him/her develop a process of elimination (getting rid of any answer choices that are incorrect).
• Make sure your child looks at **each** answer choice.
• Test-takers receive points for the number of correct answers. If your child says that (s)he does not know the answer, (s)he should first eliminate any answers that are obviously not correct. Guess instead of leaving a question unanswered.
• Remind your child to choose only ONE answer.
• Remember common sense tips like getting enough sleep. It has been scientifically proven that kids perform below their grade level when they are tired. Feed them a breakfast for sustained energy and concentration (complex carbohydrates and protein; avoid foods/drinks high in sugar). Have them use the restroom prior to the test.

THE "GIFTED DETECTIVE AGENCY"
To increase engagement and to add an incentive to complete exercises, a detective theme accompanies this book. The book's characters belong to a detective agency. They want your child to help them solve "puzzles" so that your child can join, too! As your child completes the book, allow him/her to "check" the boxes at the bottom of the Workbook and Practice Question Set pages. If your child "checks all the boxes," (s)he will "join." Feel free to modify the number of pages/exercises your child must complete in order to receive his/her certificate (p. 96).

The Gifted Detective Agency

We're the Gifted Detective Agency. We need another member, and we think YOU have what it takes to join us.

Detectives in the Gifted Detective Agency figure out puzzles and find answers to questions.

To prove you're ready to join us, you'll put your skills to the test in this book. Together with your mom, dad, or other adult, you need to solve puzzles. The adult helping you will explain what to do - listen carefully!

A good detective:
• Pays attention and listens closely
• Looks carefully at all choices before answering a question
• Keeps trying even if some questions are hard

After finishing each page, mark the box at the bottom. Like this:

Your parent (or other adult) will tell you which pages to do. After finishing them all, you will become a member of the Gifted Detective Agency! (Remember, it's more important to answer the questions the right way than to try to finish them really fast.) After you're done, you'll get your very own Gifted Detective Agency certificate.

When you're ready to start the puzzles,
write your name here: _____

QUESTION EXAMPLES & EXPLANATIONS This section introduces the 9 COGAT® question types through <u>basic</u> examples and explanations. In each question type (#1-#9), show your child the example (one basic example question consisting of images), then read the directions aloud. After the directions there are additional explanations for parents.

VERBAL BATTERY

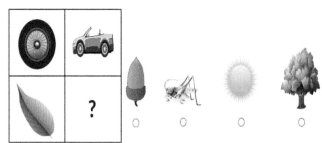

<u>1. Picture Analogies</u> Directions: The pictures in the top boxes go together in some way. Look at the bottom boxes. One is empty. Next to the boxes is a row of pictures. Which one goes with the picture in the bottom box like the pictures in the top boxes do?

Explanation Your child must determine how the top set is related. Then, (s)he must determine what answer choice goes in the box with a question mark so that the bottom set has the same relationship as the top. It's helpful to come up with a "rule" describing how the top set goes together. Take this rule, apply it to the bottom picture and determine which answer choice makes the bottom set follow the same "rule." If more than one choice works, then you need a more specific rule.

Here is a tire and a car. A tire is part of a car. A tire is found on a car. A rule would be, "the thing in the first box is found on the thing in the second box. The first thing is part of the second thing." On the bottom is a leaf. Try the answer choices with the rule. An acorn is not correct because a leaf is not part of an acorn, nor is a leaf found on a grasshopper, nor on the sun. A tree is correct because a leaf is found on a tree. A leaf is part of a tree.

These simple examples are an introduction to common analogy logic. Read the "Question" then "Answer Choices" to your child. Which choice goes best? Note that all logic is *reversible*. For example, "Part: Whole" could also be "Whole: Part."

<u>Analogy Logic</u>	<u>Questions</u>	<u>Answer Choices (Answer is Underlined)</u>			
• "X": Opposite of "X"	On *is to* Off -as- Hot *is to* ?	Warm	Sun	<u>Cold</u>	Oven
• Part: Whole	Toe *is to* Foot -as- Petal *is to* ?	Stem	Bee	Leg	<u>Flower</u>
• Animal: Its Home	Bird *is to* Nest -as- Bat *is to* ?	<u>Cave</u>	Fly	Night	Wing
• Animal: Its Food	Seed *is to* Bird -as- Acorn *is to* ?	Nut	Peanut	<u>Squirrel</u>	Worm
• Animal: Its Covering	Bird *is to* Feathers -as- Fish *is to* ?	Swim	Sharks	Tails	<u>Scales</u>
• Baby: Adult	Duckling *is to* Duck -as- Chick *is to* ?	Goose	<u>Rooster</u>	Egg	Hatch
• Object: Item Used to Consume It	Soup *is to* Spoon -as- Drink *is to* ?	Liquid	Juice	Fork	<u>Straw</u>
• Vehicle: Worker	Police Car *is to* Police Officer -as- Spaceship *is to* ?	Rocket	Planet	<u>Astronaut</u>	Doctor
• Object: Location	Sun *is to* Sky -as- Swing *is to* ?	<u>Playground</u>	Monkey Bars	Fun	Up
• Similar: Similar	Turkey *is to* Parrot -as- Ant *is to* ?	Worm	<u>Beetle</u>	Duck	Crawl
• Food: Its Source	Honey *is to* Bee -as- Egg *is to* ?	Farm	Beehive	Round	<u>Chicken</u>
• Object: Creator	Painting *is to* Artist -as- Furniture *is to* ?	<u>Carpenter</u>	Tool	Chair	Potter
• Object: Container	Ice Cube *is to* Ice Tray -as- Flower *is to* ?	Petal	<u>Vase</u>	Smell	Florist
• Tool: Worker	Paintbrush *is to* Artist -as- Microscope *is to* ?	Telescope	<u>Scientist</u>	Lab	Fireman
• Object: Its Shape	Ball *is to* Sphere -as- Dice *is to* ?	Line	Oval	<u>Cube</u>	Cone
• Object: Action You Do When Using It	Microphone *is to* Talk -as- Binoculars *is to* ?	Hear	Speak	Spell	<u>See</u>
• Whole: Part (Materials to Make a Home)	Anthill *is to* Dirt -as- Cabin *is to* ?	<u>Wood</u>	House	Person	Sand
• Object: Location (Vehicles)	Jet *is to* Sky -as- Canoe *is to* ?	Boat	Land	<u>Water</u>	Sail
• Object: Where It's Used	Chalk *is to* Chalkboard -as- Paintbrush *is to* ?	Artist	<u>Easel</u>	Museum	Eraser

<u>2. Picture Classification</u> Directions: The top row shows pictures that are alike in some way. Look at the bottom row. Which bottom picture goes best with those on top?

Explanation Come up with a "rule" describing how they're alike. Then, see which answer choice follows the rule. If more than one choice does, then try a more specific rule.

Here are shoes, gloves, and dice. At first, it may be hard to see anything they have in common. Let's look closer. They each show a pair. This is how they are alike. The first and second pictures do not show a pair (a fan and bubble mix). The last choice, ice cream scoops, shows three scoops, not two. The third choice shows the correct answer – a pair of socks. Everyday life presents an opportunity to improve classification skills, as themes for Picture Classification (and Picture Analogies and Sentence Completion) include (but are not limited to) this list of common classification logic (gray font). Under the logic is an example question. Read the first list of 3 words to your child. Then, next to it, read the 4 choices to your child. Which one of the choices goes best with the first list?

• function and uses of common objects (i.e., writing and drawing / measuring / cutting / drinking / eating)
Fork / Chopsticks / Knife   Choices: Stove / Kitchen / Meat / <u>Spoon</u>   (Used For Eating)
• location of common objects
Refrigerator / Cabinet / Table   Choices: Bed / Restaurant / <u>Oven</u> / Shower   (Found In Kitchens)
• appearance of common objects (i.e., color; objects in pairs; objects with stripes vs. spots; object's shape)
Ketchup / Blood / Firetruck   Choices: <u>Cherry</u> / Mustard / Cucumber / Police car   (Red)
• characteristics of common objects (i.e., hot, cold)
Ice / Igloo / Popsicle   Choices: Cookie / <u>Snowman</u> / Palm Tree / Coffee   (Cold)
• animal/human homes
Aquarium / Barn / Nest   Choices: Feather / <u>Beehive</u> / Farmer / Fish   (Animal Homes)
• animal types
Leopard / Cheetah / Kitten   Choices: Elephant / Giraffe / <u>Tiger</u> / Bat   (Cats)
• natural habitats
Swamp / River / Pond   Choices: Desert / Mountain / House / <u>Ocean</u>   (Water)
• food types
Cake / Bread / Donut   Choices: Sherbet / <u>Cookie</u> / Syrup / Sugar   (Baked Foods)
• food growing location (i.e., on a tree, under the ground as a root, or on a vine)
Potato / Carrot / Onion   Choices: <u>Radish</u> / Melon / Pepper / Broccoli   (Root Vegetables)
• professions, community helpers
Doctor / Fireman / Vet   Choices: Witch / Wizard / <u>Teacher</u> / Baby   (Community Helpers)
• clothing (i.e., in what weather it's worn; on what body part it's worn)
Crown / Cowboy Hat / Cap   Choices: Necklace / <u>Helmet</u> / Gloves / Ring   (Worn On Head)
• transportation (i.e., where things travel, land/water/air; do they have wheels?)
Cruise Ship / Yacht / Kayak   Choices: <u>Canoe</u> / Fisherman / Dock / Jeep   (Travel On Water)

Additional topics include seasons and weather, sports objects, basic solar system knowledge (i.e., about the sun, moon, Earth), appearance of animal babies vs. adults, and musical instruments.

3. Sentence Completion   Directions: Listen to the question, then choose your answer. (Each question has different directions.) Max sees something floating in the water. Which one does Max see?

Explanation   The first choice, a rock, doesn't float, neither does a hammer or a coin. A beach ball does float in water; it is the answer. Your child must listen carefully. Test administrators will read the question only one time. To practice listening, remind your child to listen to **all** directions, from start to finish. Some kids stop paying attention when they think they know the answer. Build knowledge related to the list of themes in Picture Classification (which also helps with Picture Analogies).

NONVERBAL BATTERY

4. Figure Analogies   Directions: The pictures inside the top boxes go together in some way. Look at the bottom boxes. One is empty. Next to the boxes is a row of pictures. Which one goes with the picture in the bottom box like the pictures in the top boxes? (The word "picture" here actually refers to a "figure" that can consist of shapes, lines, etc.)

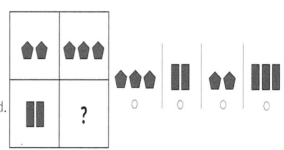

Explanation   Come up with a "rule" describing how the top set is related. This shows how the left box "changes" into the right box. On the left are 2 pentagons. On the right are 3 pentagons. The rule/change is that one more of the same kind of shape was added. On the bottom are 2 rectangles. The first choice is incorrect because it shows 3 pentagons - not the same shapes as the bottom box. The second choice is incorrect - it only shows 2 rectangles. The third choice is incorrect - it has 2 pentagons. The last choice is correct - there are 3 rectangles (1 more of the same shapes that were in the left box).

Here's a list of frequent "rules" / "changes" in Figure Analogies. Easier questions involve one "change," while more challenging questions involve more than one change (see example #9 below).

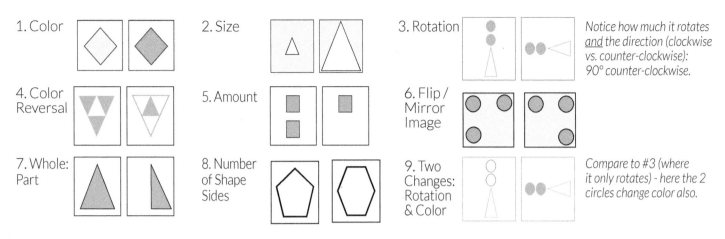

1. Color

2. Size

3. Rotation — Notice how much it rotates *and* the direction (clockwise vs. counter-clockwise): 90° counter-clockwise.

4. Color Reversal

5. Amount

6. Flip / Mirror Image

7. Whole: Part

8. Number of Shape Sides

9. Two Changes: Rotation & Color — Compare to #3 (where it only rotates) - here the 2 circles change color also.

5. Figure Classification Directions: Look at the top row of pictures. These pictures are alike in some way. Look at the bottom row. Which picture on the bottom goes best with the pictures on top?

Explanation The "pictures" in the directions refer to figures. Try to come up with a "rule" describing how the figures in the top row are alike. Then, see which choice follows the rule. If more than one choice would, then a more specific rule is needed. Here is 1 white triangle, 1 lightly shaded triangle, and 1 dark triangle. These are alike because they are all triangles. The first choice is correct because it's a triangle. None of the other choice (B, C, D) are triangles. If you get "stumped" by any of these, then try asking these kinds of questions:

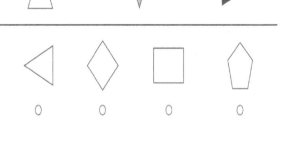

- If there are 3 main figures (above), how many sides do they have?
- If there are 3 main figures, are they made of straight lines or are they rounded?
- If there are 3 main figures, are the shapes flat or 3-D?
- What direction are the figures facing?
- If the figures are different colors or if the figures have dots/lines inside, what do these look like?
- If the figures are divided, how are they divided?
- If each of the 3 figures is actually made of a group of shapes, how many shapes are in the group?
- If each of the 3 figures is actually made of a group of shapes, where are the shapes within the group?
- If each of the 3 figures is actually made of a group of shapes, is there a particular order of the group of shapes?

6. Paper Folding Directions: The top row of pictures shows a sheet of paper, how it was folded, and how something was cut out of it. Which picture on the bottom row shows how the paper would look after its unfolded?

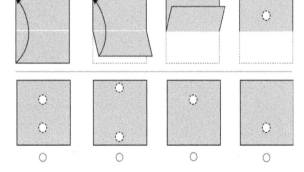

Explanation The first choice shows how it would look - 2 holes in the correct position. In the second choice, the holes are too close to the edge. In the third and fourth choice, there's only 1 hole. (Even though you only see 1 hole in the top row, when the paper is unfolded, there will be 2.) Here, holes have been cut out. However, other questions have different shapes cut out. Also, some questions will show paper that has been folded more than once.

Pay attention to: the number of objects cut out, where these objects are on the paper, and the direction they are facing. Try demonstrating with real paper. For example, you could do the first few Paper Folding questions (starting on p.32) using real paper and a hole puncher or scissors. Seeing real-life examples will assist children with correctly envisioning the paper folding steps during the test.

QUANTITATIVE BATTERY

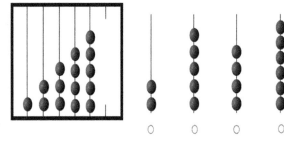

7. <u>Number Series</u> Directions: Which rod would go in the place of the missing rod to finish the pattern?

Explanation The last abacus rod is missing. Before it, the rods have made a pattern that your child must figure out. Then, "complete" the pattern with the correct answer choice. Young kids will frequently miscount the beads, so first, ensure they are correctly counting the beads. Looking across the abacus, from left to right, we see that with each rod the number of beads increases by 1. The rods go: 1-2-3-4-5- ? This means that the missing rod needs 6 beads (Choice D).
Here is a list of common logic patterns found in Number Series questions. This book has examples of all of these.

Logic	Number of Beads		Logic	Number of Beads
1 bead is added	(0, 1, 2, 3, 4)		1 bead is taken away	(5, 4, 3, 2, 1)
2 beads are added	(0, 2, 4, 6, 8)		2 beads are taken away	(6, 4, 2, 0)
A-A-B-A-A-B	(3, 3, 2, 3, 3, 2)		A-B-C	(3, 2, 1, 3, 2, 1)
A-A-B-B-C-C	(3, 3, 2, 2, 1, 1)		A-B-C-zero-C-B-A	(6-3-2-0-2-3-6)

A / X / A+1 / X / A+2	(1, 0, 2, 0, 3, 0, 4)	(here "X" is 0, it gets repeated every other time)
A / X / A-1 / X / A-2	(8, 1, 7, 1, 6, 1, 5)	(here "X" is 1, it gets repeated every other time)
A / B / A+1 / B+1 / A+2 / B+2	(1, 5, 2, 6, 3, 7)	(the first, third, fifth number & the second, fourth, sixth number increase by 1)
A / B / A-1 / B-1 / A-2 / B-2	(7, 3, 6, 2, 5, 1)	(the first, third, fifth number & the second, fourth, sixth number decrease by 1)

8. <u>Number Puzzles</u> Directions: Which train car goes in the box with the question mark so that the bottom train has the same number of things as the top train?

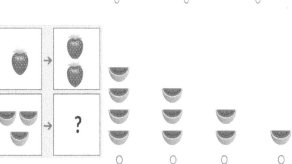

Explanation The top train has 4 things. The bottom train has 1 thing. The train on the top must have the same total number of things as the one on the bottom. Make sure to carefully and correctly count the number of things. We need 3 things in the train car with the question mark to have a total of 4 things in the bottom train. One thing in the train car on the left plus three from the train car on the right equals four things (1 + 3 = 4.) Ensure (s)he correctly counts the objects in the train cars. You may want to practice writing down the numbers each car has next to it - so as not to forget. To double check that (s)he answers questions correctly, you may want to have your child check if each answer choice works. Practice basic math equations together to build skills.

9. <u>Number Analogies</u> Directions: The pictures on top go together in some way. Look at the bottom boxes. One is empty. Next to the boxes is a row of pictures. Which choice goes with the bottom box like the pictures on top do?

Explanation Number Analogies are similar to Picture/Figure Analogies, but now the top set and the bottom set must have the same mathematical relationship. In the left box there is 1 object (a strawberry). In the right box there are 2 objects. From left to right, we see that 1 object has been added. So, the rule here is "1 is added" or "+1." In the bottom left box there are 3 objects. If our rule is "1 is added," when you have 3 and you add 1, you get 4. (3 + 1 = 4.) Choice A is the correct answer. Many of these questions involve basic addition and subtraction. However, some questions will involve dividing a group of objects (p.46 #7), as well as basic halving (p.48 #12) and basic doubling (p.47 #11).

Tip: If you think a rule is to add or subtract on top, and find that none of the answer choices work with the bottom left box, then you try to double (if the top boxes increase from left to right) or halve (if the top boxes decrease from left to right). On the left, from the top boxes, you may have the rule "take away 2" (4 - 2 = 2). However, 6 - 2 = 4, but there is no answer choice with 4. Half of 4 is 2. Half of 6 is 3 (Choice C).

ANYA NEEDS YOUR HELP TO FIGURE OUT WHICH PICTURE DOESN'T BELONG!

Directions: Look at this row of pictures. One of these pictures in the row does not belong. This picture is not like the others in the row. Which picture does not belong?

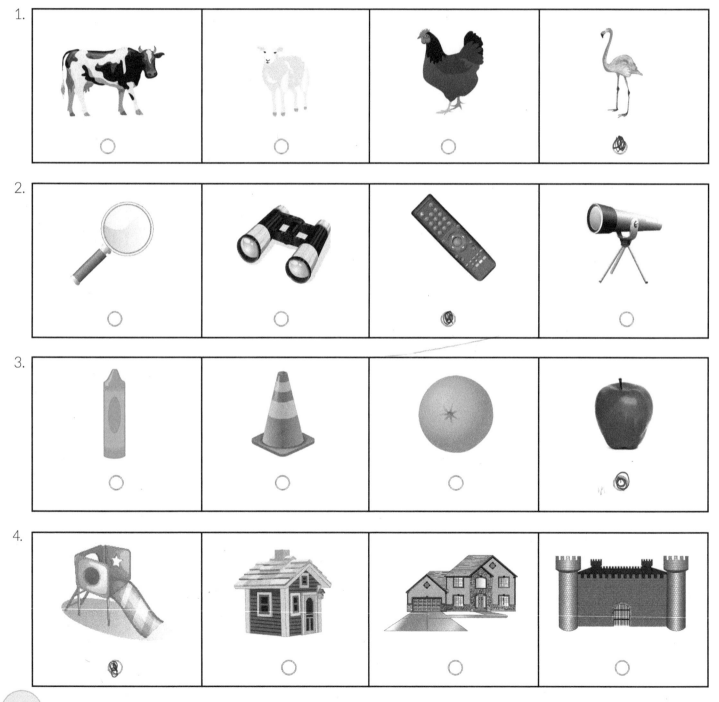

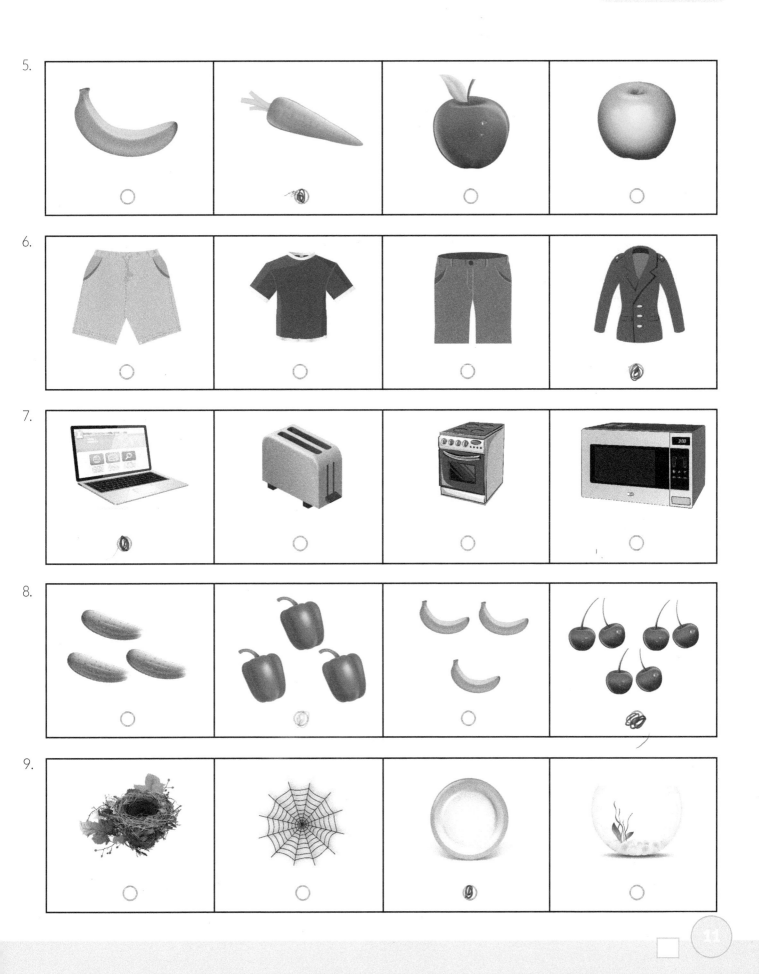

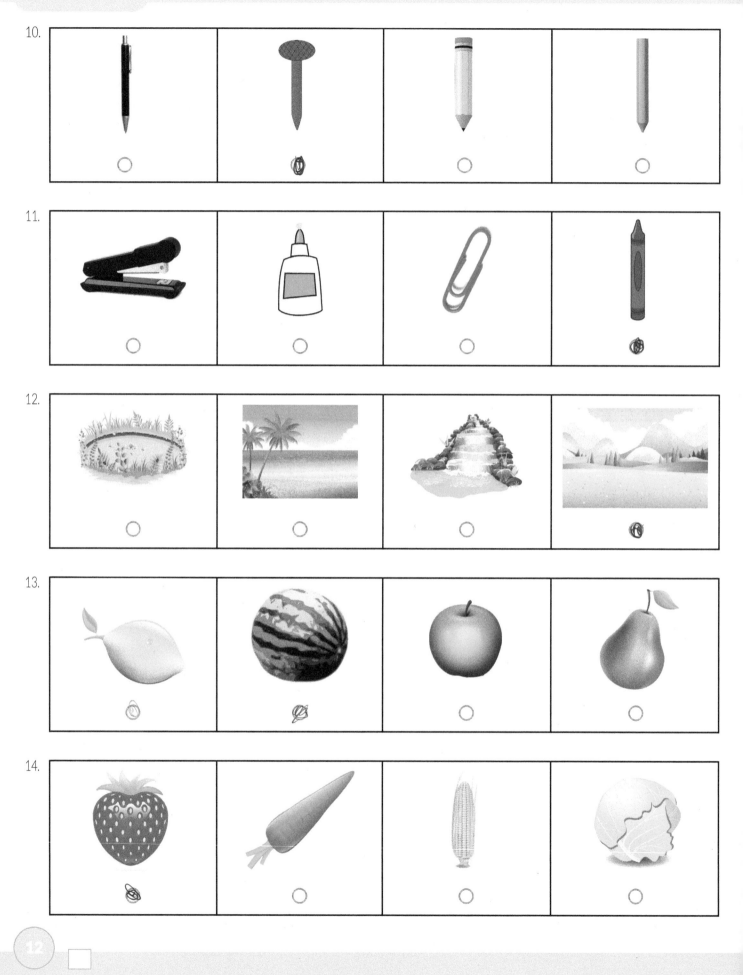

MAY SAYS, "YOU'RE DOING GREAT!" NOW, LET'S DO THE SAME THING WITH SHAPES.

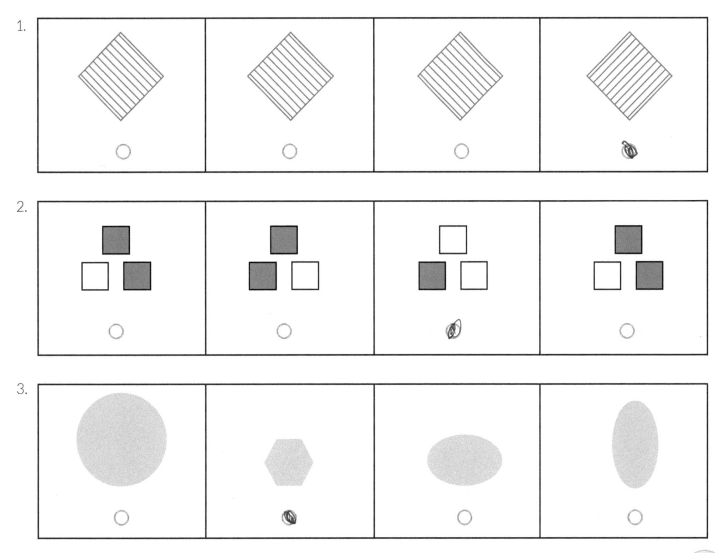

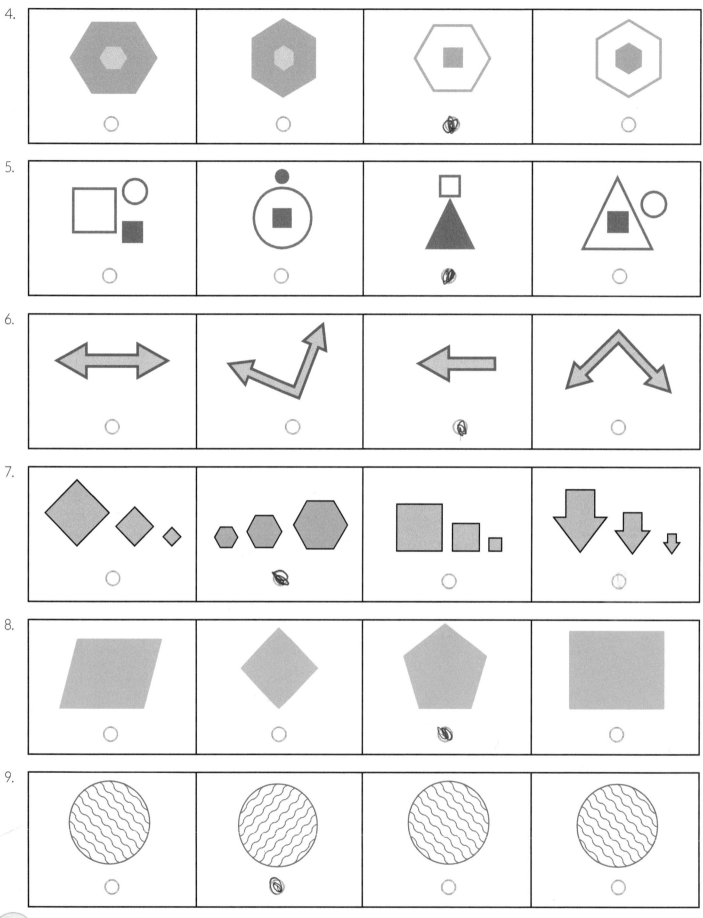

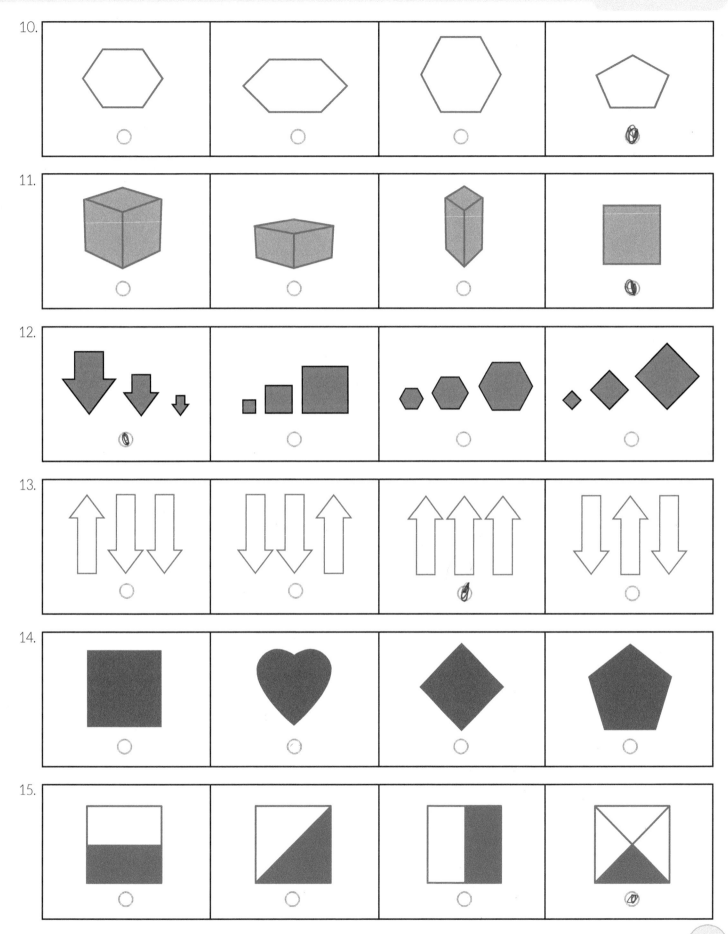

LET'S HELP FREDDIE FIGURE OUT WHAT GOES IN THE EMPTY BOX!

Directions: Look at these boxes that are on top. The pictures that are inside belong together in some way.

Then, look at these boxes that are on the bottom. One of these boxes on the bottom is empty.

Look next to the boxes. There is a row of pictures. Which one would go together with this picture that is in the bottom box like these pictures that are in the top boxes?

Parent note: Analogies compare sets of items, and the way they are related can easily be missed at first. Work through these together with your child so (s)he sees how the top set is related. Together, try to come up with a "rule" to describe how the top set is related. (The small arrows show that the pictures belong together in some way.) Then, look at the picture on the bottom. Take this "rule," use it together with the picture on the bottom, and figure out which of the answer choices would follow that same rule. For answer choices that do not follow this rule, eliminate them. If your child finds that more than one choice follows this rule, then try to come up with a rule that is more specific.

Example (read this to your child): Look at the boxes on top. In the first box there is a spaceship (or, rocket). In the second box there is an astronaut. (Talk about the two pictures and try to come up with a "rule.") An astronaut travels in a spaceship. The astronaut must ride in the spaceship to do his/her job. What is in the bottom box? It is a fire truck. Now, let's look at the answer choices. Which one goes with the picture of the fire truck in the same way that the pictures in the top row go together? A firefighter! A firefighter travels in a fire truck and rides in it to do his/her job.

1.

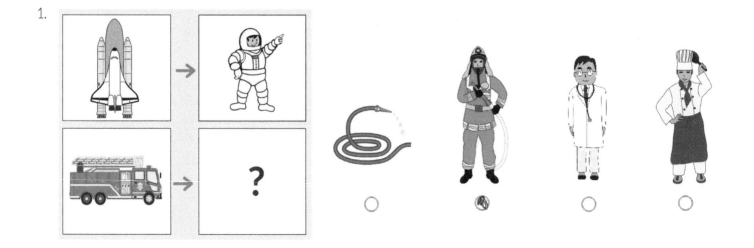

2.

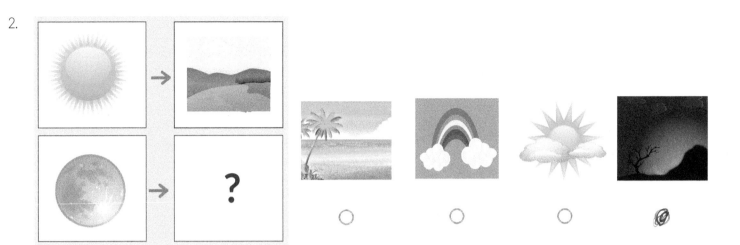

3.

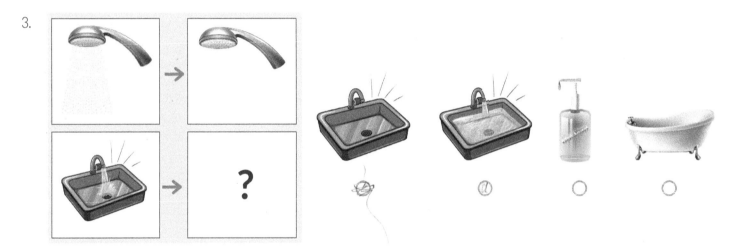

4.

5.

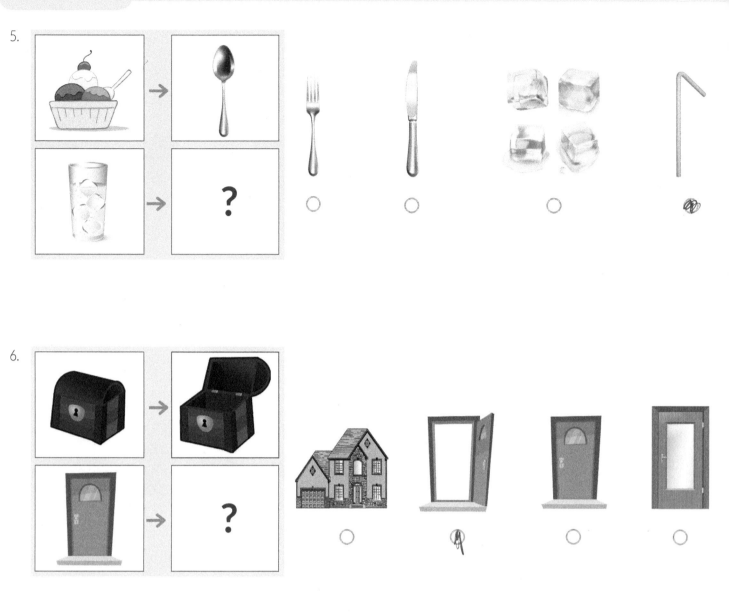

6.

7.

8.

9.

10.

Let's help Anya with the same kind of questions on the next pages, but now we'll use shapes!

Parent Note: As you did with Picture Analogies, together, come up with a "rule" to describe how the top set is related. With Figure Analogies, often this rule will describe how the picture in the left box "changes" into the picture in the right box.

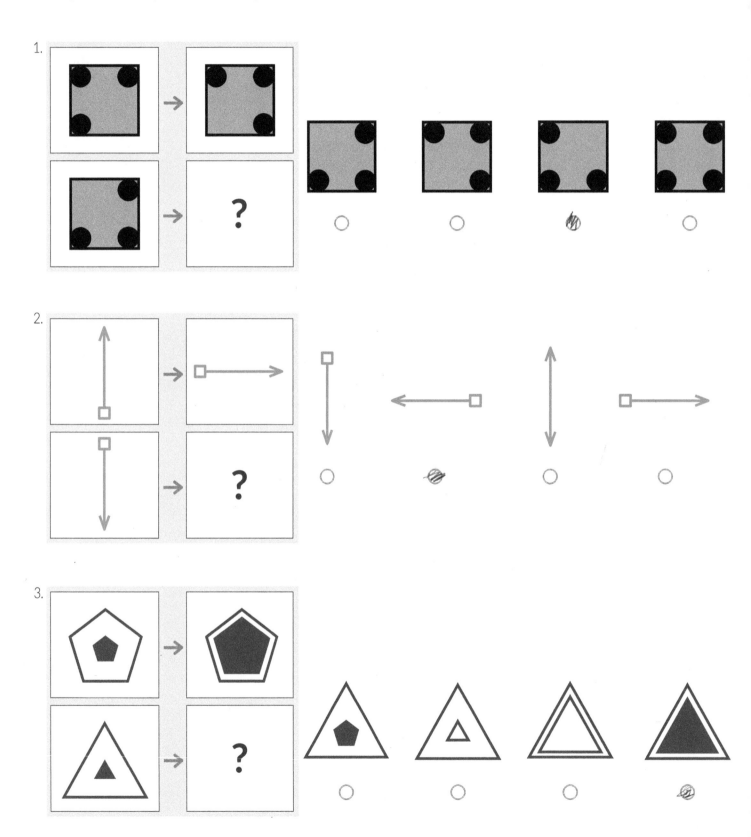

1.

2.

3.

4.

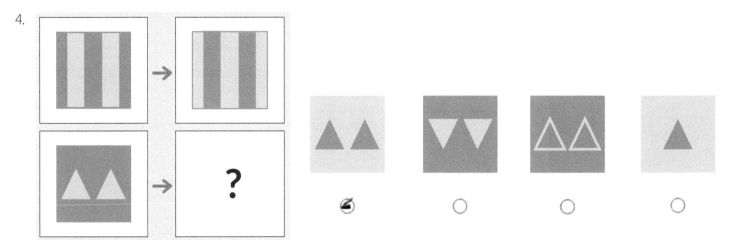

5.

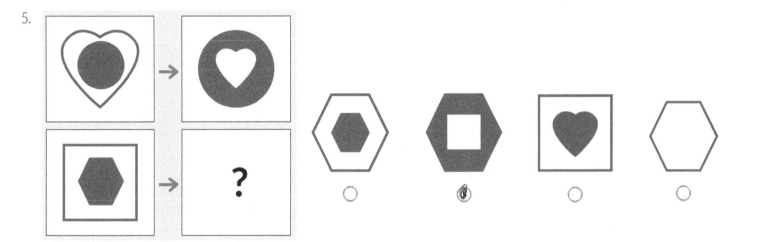

6.

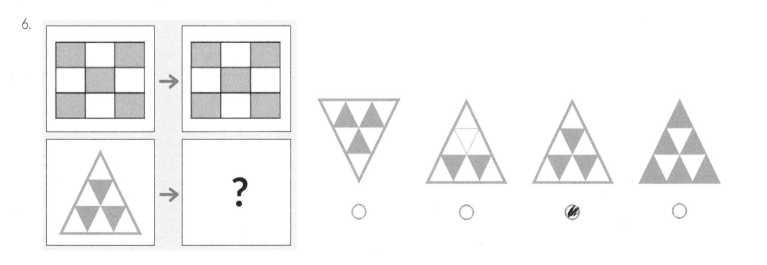

WILL YOU HELP SOPHIE ANSWER THESE?

Directions: Look at the top row of pictures. These pictures are alike in a certain way. Then, look at the pictures that are on the bottom row. Which picture that is in the bottom row would go best with the pictures that are in the top row?

Example (read this to your child): Let's look at the top row of pictures. We see a book, a microwave oven, and an umbrella. Let's come up with a "rule" to describe how they each are alike. Let's look at them carefully. The book is open. The microwave is open. The umbrella is open. Let's look at the bottom row. We need to find the answer on the bottom that follows the same rule. We see a door, a box, an envelope, and eyes. Which one of these goes best with the pictures in the top row? The eyes! The door, the box, and the envelope are closed. The eyes are open.

Parent note: As with the analogies questions, when your child finds answer choices that do not follow the "rule," (s)he should eliminate them. If your child finds that more than one choice follows the rule, then (s)he should try to come up with a rule that is more specific.

1.

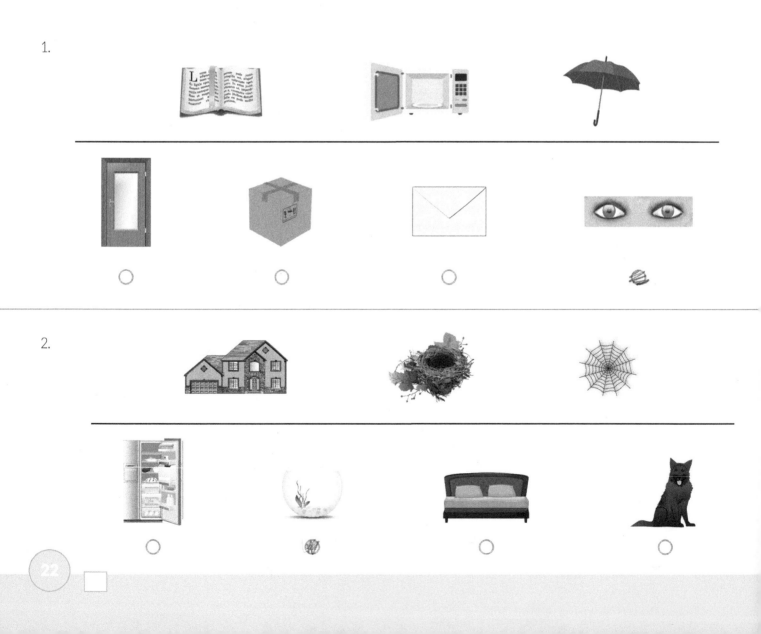

2.

3.

4.

5.

6.

7.

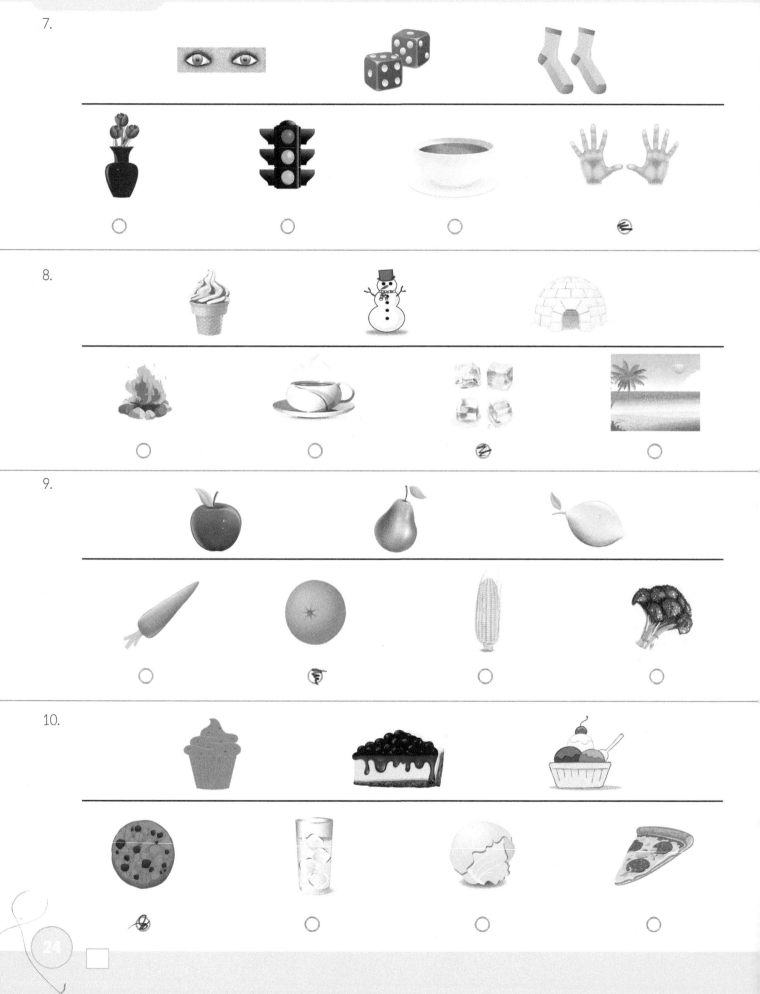

8.

9.

10.

11.

12.

13.

14.

Freddie needs more help - this time using shapes.
Which picture on the bottom row goes best with the pictures in the top row?

1.

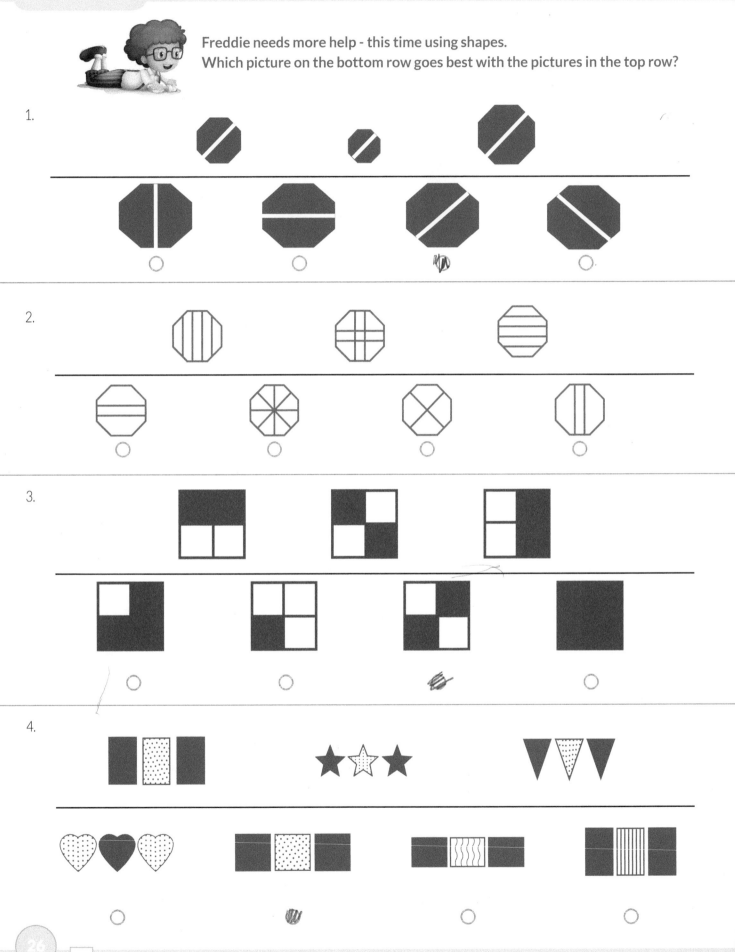

2.

3.

4.

5.

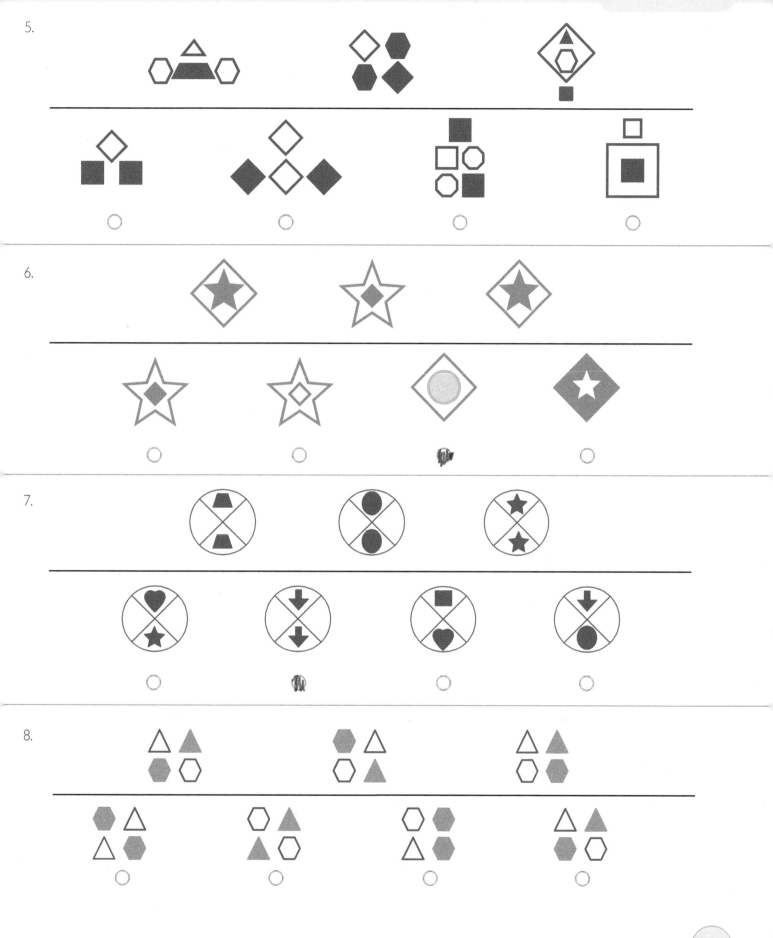

6.

7.

8.

LET'S HELP ANYA AND ALEX ANSWER THESE QUESTIONS.

Directions: Listen to the question and then choose your answer.

Parent Note: These exercises are similar to those on the Sentence Completion section of the COGAT®. Try to read each question only one time to your child so that (s)he can practice listening skills.

1. Which one of these foods is juicy?

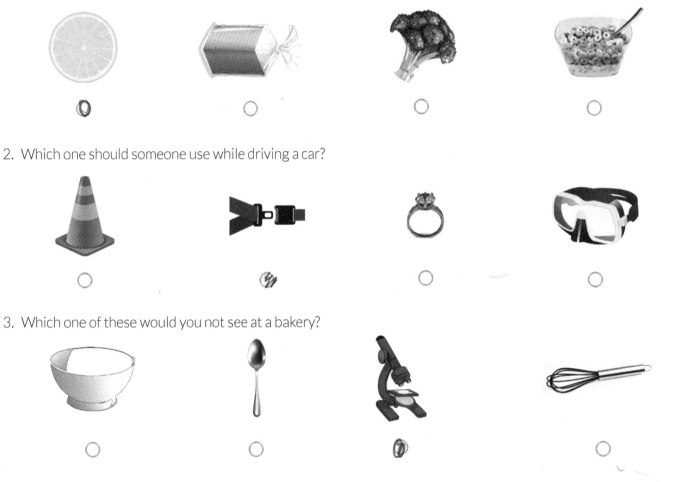

2. Which one should someone use while driving a car?

3. Which one of these would you not see at a bakery?

4. Which one of these would you board inside a subway station?

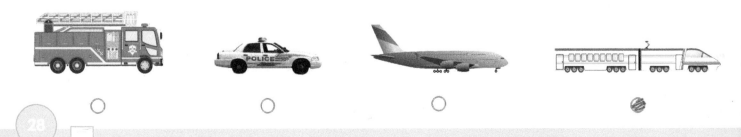

5. Which of these would not work at a beach?

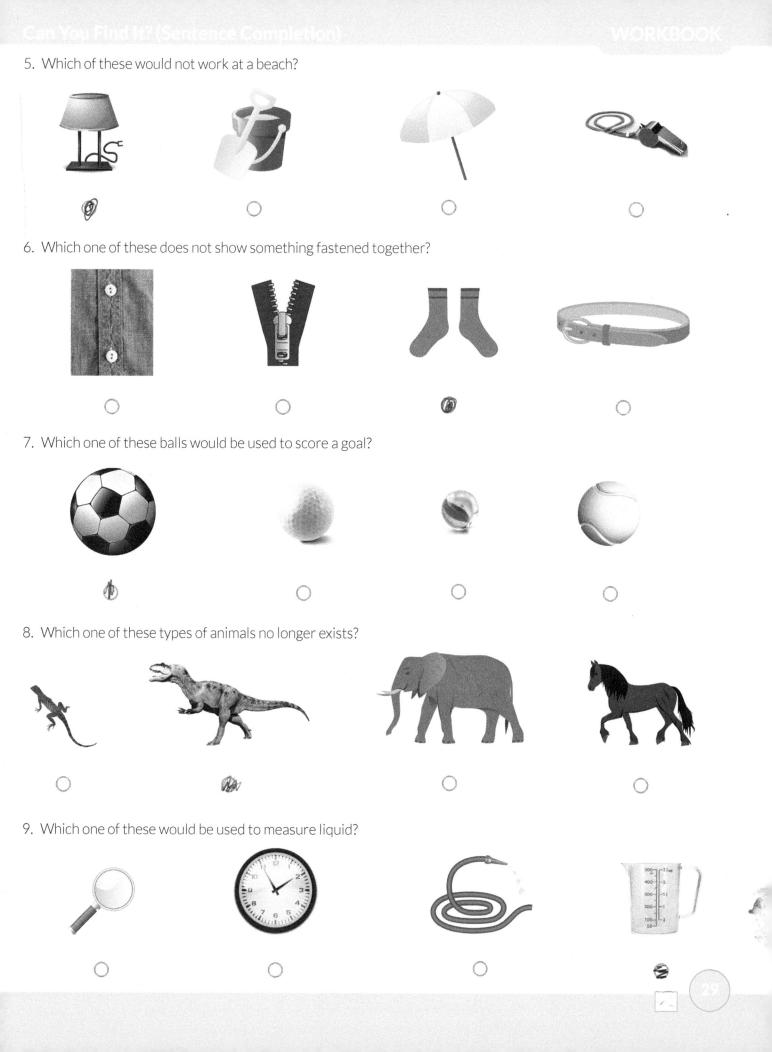

6. Which one of these does not show something fastened together?

7. Which one of these balls would be used to score a goal?

8. Which one of these types of animals no longer exists?

9. Which one of these would be used to measure liquid?

10. If someone said that they could hear an animal howling, which animal would they be hearing?

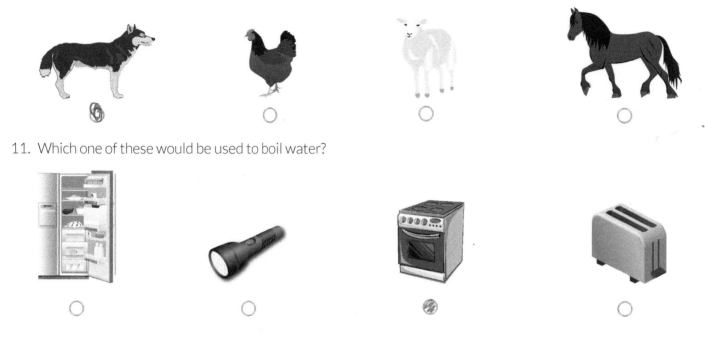

11. Which one of these would be used to boil water?

12. Look at this picture at the beginning of the row. It is made of numbers, letters, and shapes. Next to the picture are the answer choices. Which one of the choices shows the number that is beside a triangle and below the letter "J"?

8	■	5	▲
R	2	●	▲
▲	J	K	B
M	3	▲	■

2   3   5   M

13. Look at this picture at the beginning of the row. It shows an apple, a pizza, and a cookie. Which answer choice shows this: half of an apple, a pizza that is still whole, and half of a cookie?

14. Which picture shows this: Max is standing up between a bike and a tree? There are two birds are under the tree.

15. Which picture shows this: two stars at opposite ends of the line and a white circle inside a gray square in the middle?

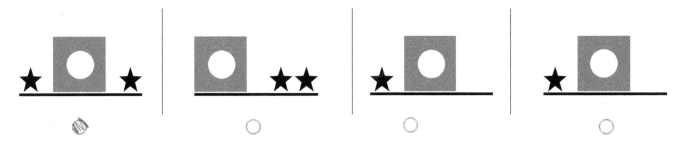

16. Sophie read a book about an animal that cannot breathe under the water and it cannot fly. Which animal was Sophie's book about?

17. Max's 2 favorite foods are something that's caught from a boat and something that is picked from a tree. Which picture shows Max's 2 favorite foods?

18. To finish a project, Anya needs something to write with and something else to cut with. Which picture shows what Anya needs?

19. Which choice shows 1 living thing and 1 non-living thing?

LET'S GIVE SOPHIE A HAND!

Directions: Look at the top row of pictures. These show a sheet of paper, how it was folded, and how holes were made in the folded sheet of paper. Look at these pictures that are on the bottom row. Which picture shows how the paper would look after the paper is unfolded?

Parent note: As you go through the exercises, make sure your child pays attention to: how many times the paper is folded and the direction the shapes are pointing. The scissors on p.34 simply show where the paper was cut.

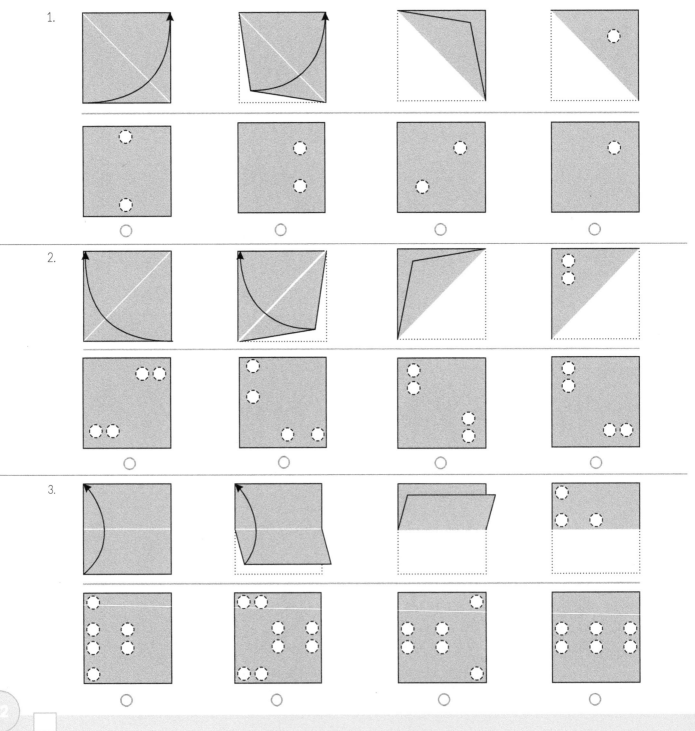

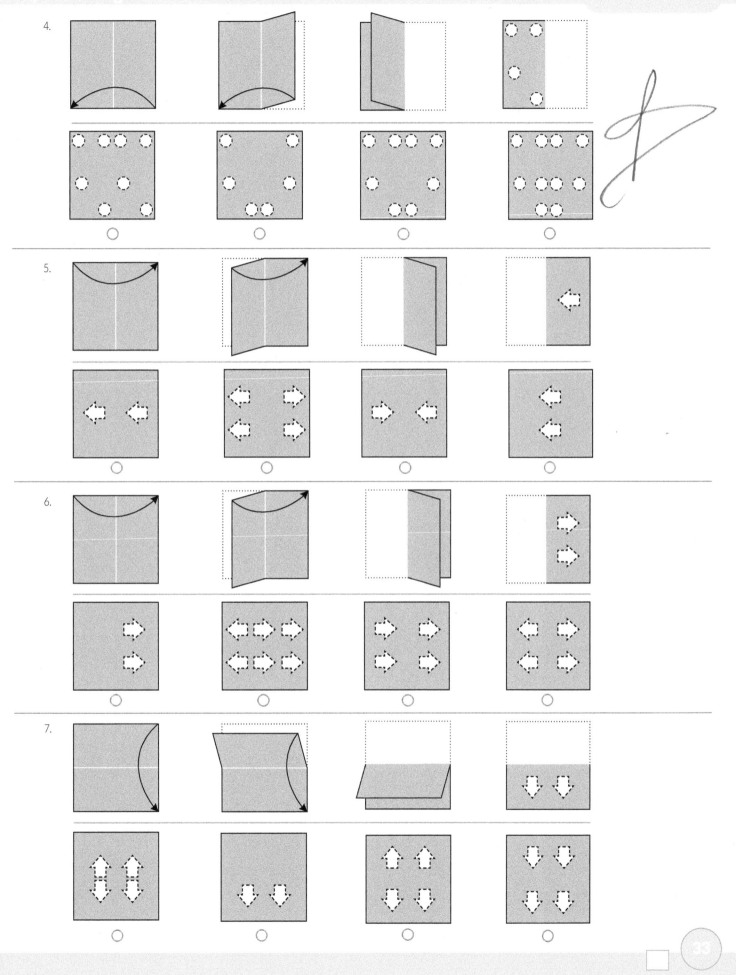

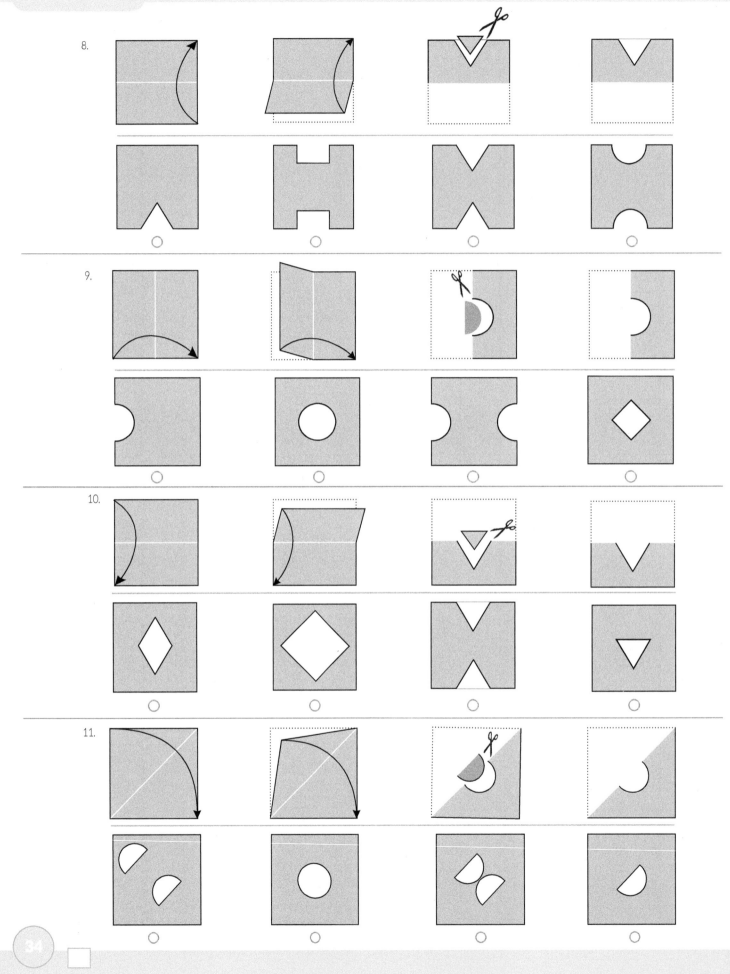

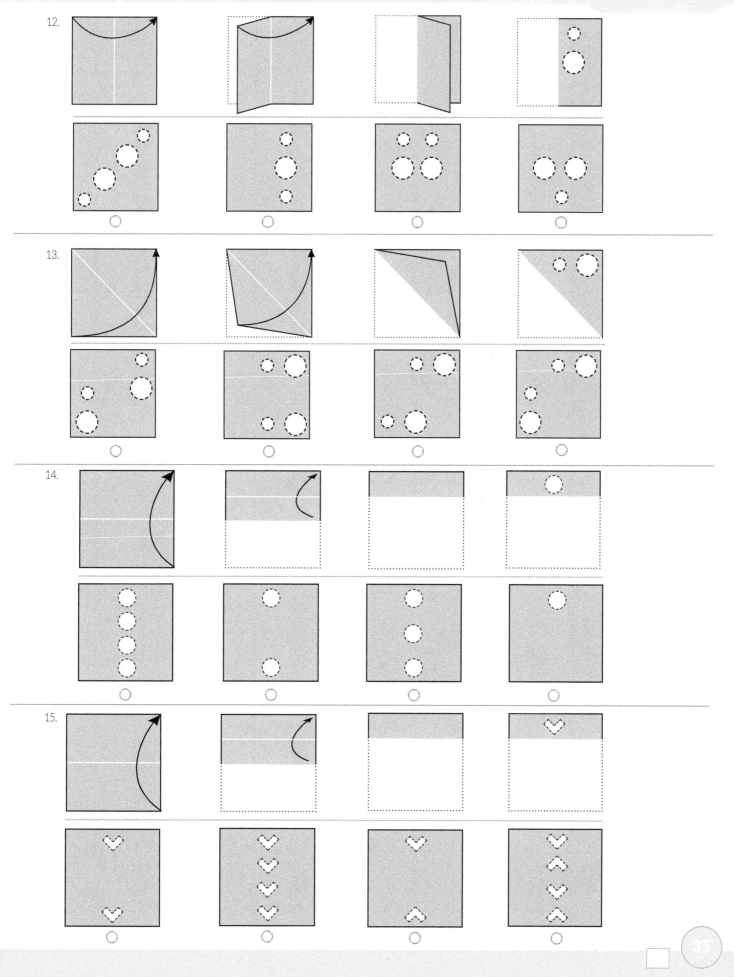

16.

17.

18.

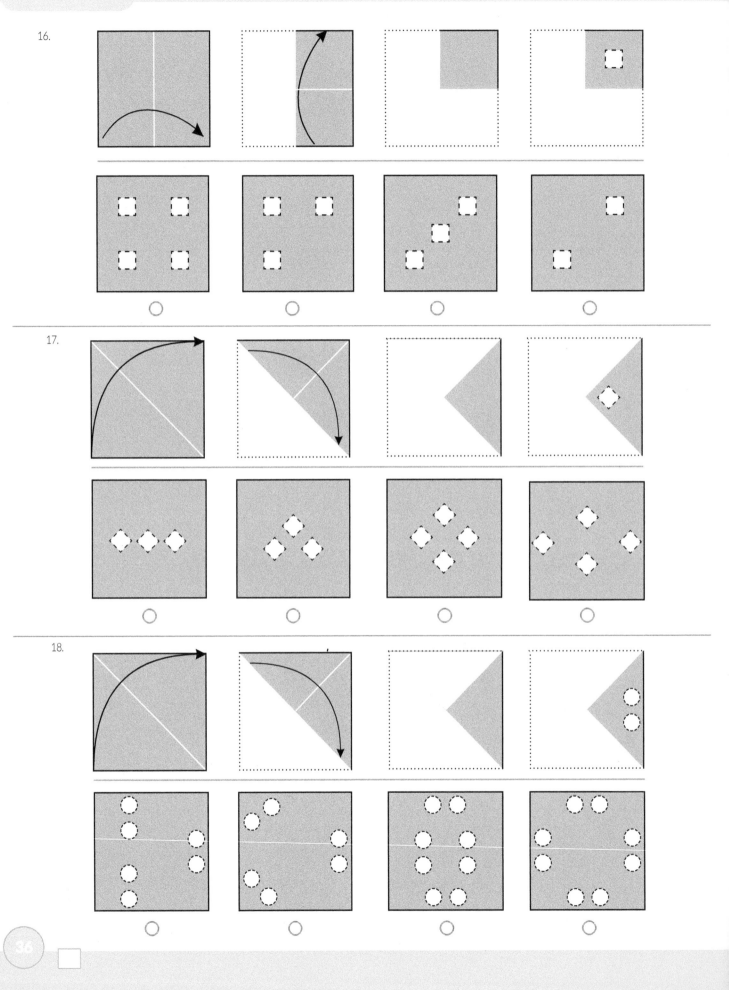

19.

20.

21.

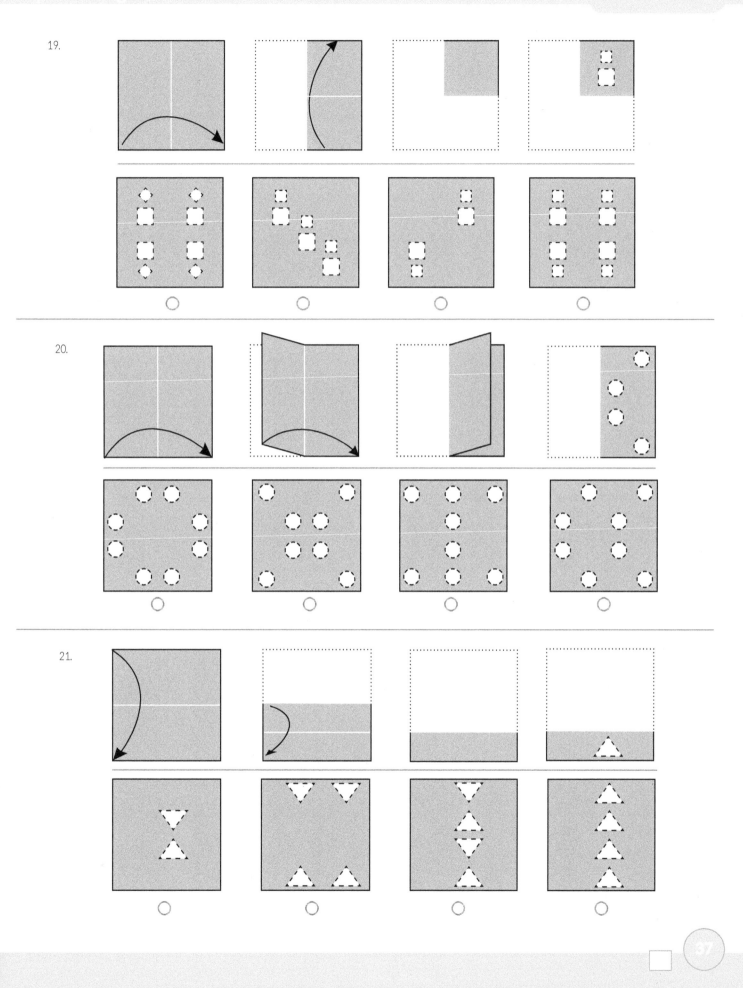

LET'S HELP MAX WITH NUMBER PUZZLES.

Section explanation: An abacus is a toy with rods and beads that is used for counting. Here, the final rod of the abacus is missing. Before the missing rod, the rods of the abacus have a pattern. Have your child look closely at these to determine the pattern. (S)he will then need to select which rod would finish the pattern. Make sure your child carefully and correctly counts the number of abacus beads. Note that some answer choices do not have any beads. This equals "0". The gray line on some rods is to facilitate counting. (Here, the questions with bead counts greater than five have these after the fifth bead.) Due to the complexity of this question type, we have included detailed directions for the first question.

Directions for first question: Here's an abacus. The "circles" on the abacus are beads. These beads are on rods. The beads in the first five rods have made a pattern. Look at the last rod on the abacus. The beads on this rod are missing. Next to the abacus are four rods. These are the answer choices. Choose which rod would go in the place of the last rod in order to complete the pattern. Let's look at the abacus. We see 7 beads, then 6 beads, then 5 beads, then 4 beads, then 3 beads. Do you see a pattern? On each rod, one bead gets taken away. What would go after the rod with 3 beads? If one bead gets taken away each time, what would go after 3 beads? The last rod on the abacus is missing. What rod goes here to finish the pattern? (Look at each answer choice.) It is the rod with 2 beads.

Directions for the rest: Which rod would go in the place of the missing rod to finish the pattern?

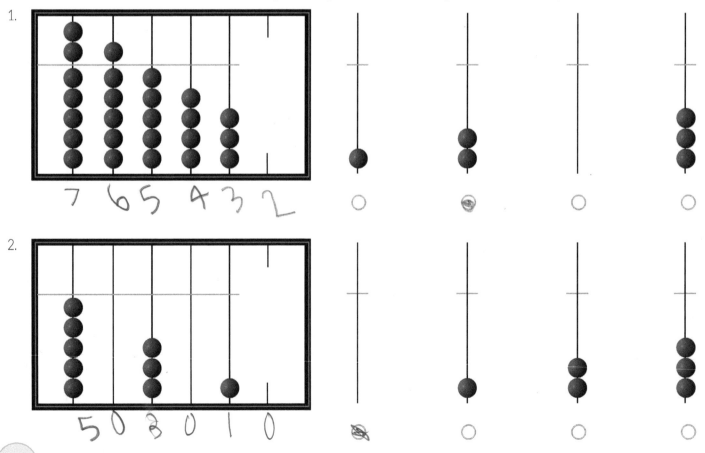

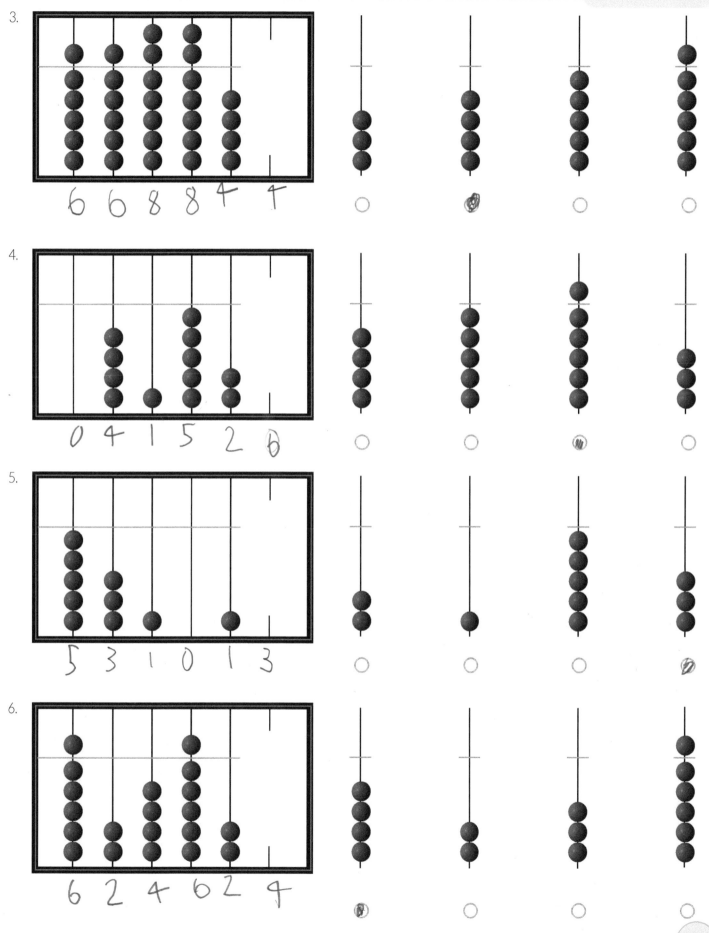

3. 6 6 8 8 4 4

4. 0 4 1 5 2 6

5. 5 3 1 0 1 3

6. 6 2 4 6 2 4

7.

8.

9.

1 3 2 4 3 5

10.

1 1 A 1 1

MAX NEEDS YOUR HELP AGAIN!

Section explanation: Here are two trains, one on the top and one on the bottom. Each train must have the same total number of things. Your child needs to figure out which answer choice would go in place of the car(s) with the question mark. The train on the top must have the same total number of things as the one on the bottom. Make sure your child carefully and correctly counts the number of things (presents or fruit, in these questions). Due to the complexity of this question type, we have included detailed directions for the first question.

Directions for first question: Look at the first train, the one on the top. It has 5 apples in the left train car and 2 apples in the right train car. Let's count the total number of apples in the top train. It's 7. Look at the train on the bottom, the second train. This train has 1 apple. You need to put a train car in place of the train car that has a question mark so that the second train has the same number of apples as the other train. Which train car should you choose so that the second train has 7 apples all together? It would be the train car that has 6 apples. One plus six equals seven. Now the two trains would have the same number of apples.

Directions for the rest: Which train car should you choose so that the second train has the same number of things as the first?

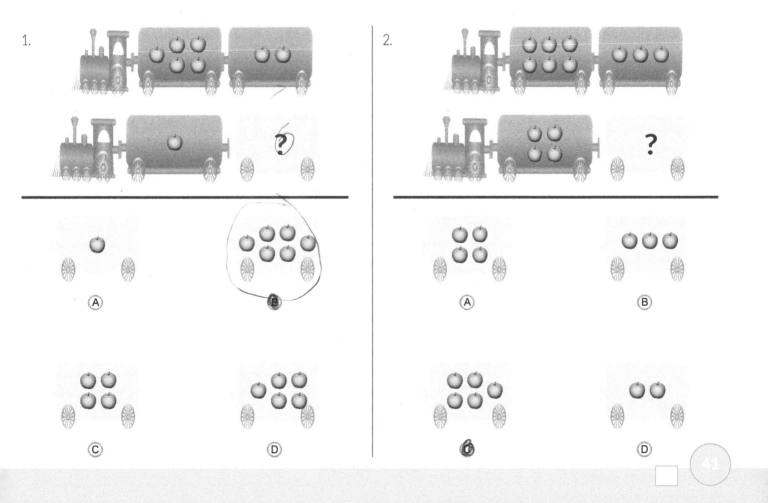

1.

2.

A   B

C   D

A   B

C   D

41

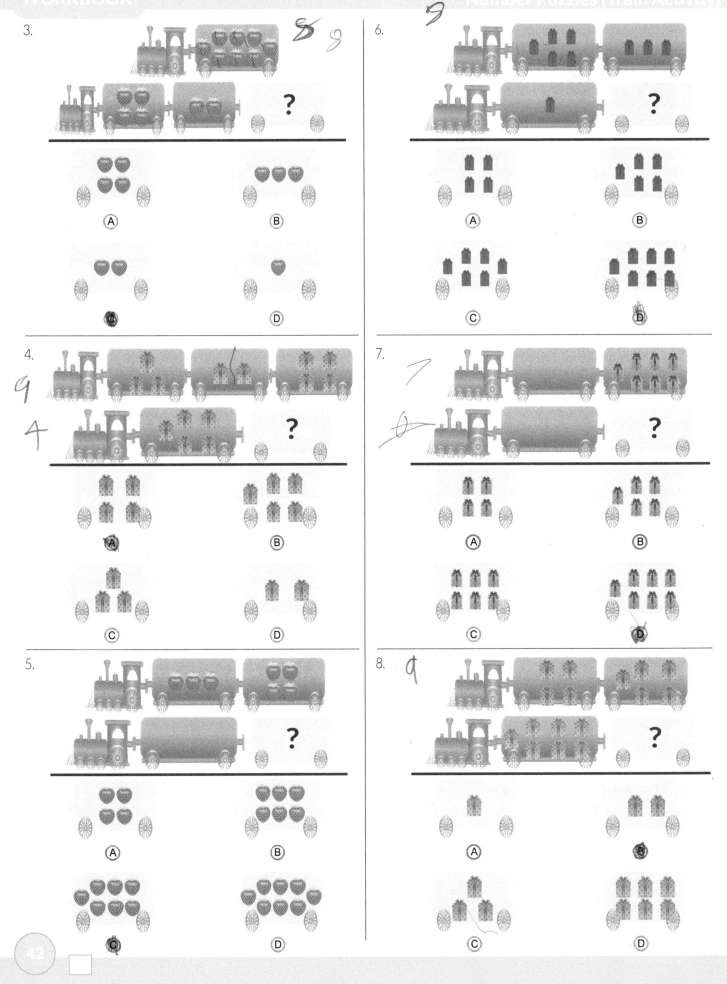

Directions for #9: Look at the train on the top. Let's count the number of presents. It's 4. Look at the train on the bottom. Let's count the number of presents. It's 5. You need to put a train car in place of the train car that has a question mark so that the second train has the same number of presents as the other train. One present must be taken away from the second train. Look at the answer choices. If something has an "X" on it, that means that it is taken away from the train. If you need to take away one present, which one would you choose? It would be the one present with the "X" on it.

Directions for the rest: Which train car should you choose so that the second train has the same number of things as the first?

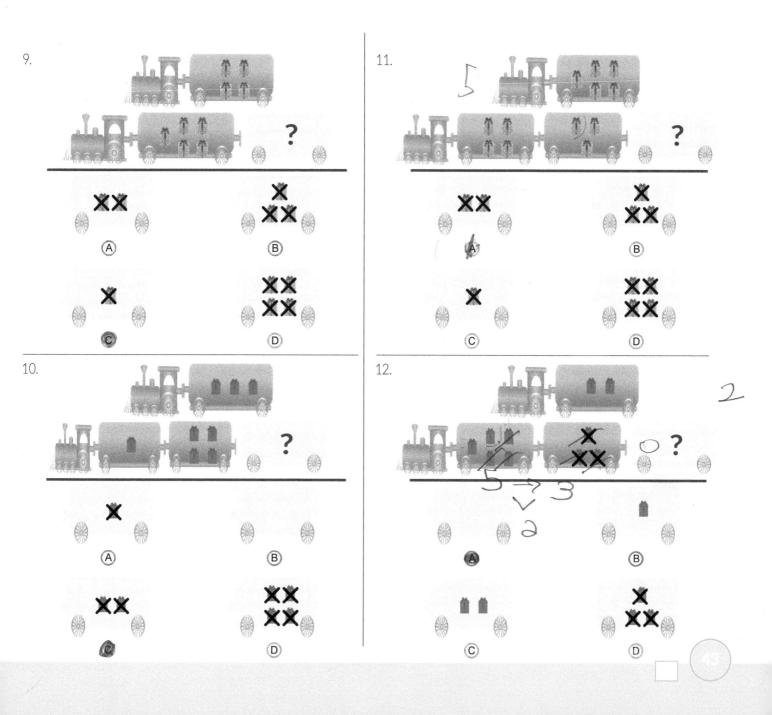

MAY NEEDS A HAND WITH NUMBER GAMES!

Section explanation: Number analogies questions are similar to the other analogies earlier in this book. Here, however, the top set of boxes and the bottom set of boxes must have the same type of quantitative relationship. Your child must figure out which one of the answer choices would go in the empty box with the question mark to complete the mathematical analogy.

Pay special attention to questions 11, 12, and 13, as these involve doubling/halving of a group of objects and not the typical addition and subtraction of earlier questions.

Due to the complexity of this section, we have included detailed directions for the first question.

Directions for first question: The top boxes belong together in some way. Look at the top box on the left - there are 8 hats. Look at the top box on the right - there are 3 hats. What has changed between the picture on the left and the picture on the right? We need to come up with a "rule" to describe what has happened. The right box has 5 less hats than the left box. Five hats were taken away to get the number of hats in the right box. Next, let's look carefully at the boxes in the bottom row. The first box has 7 hats. The second box is empty. Look carefully at the row of pictures next to the boxes. Which one of these goes in the empty box? The answer is "2 hats." On the bottom row, the first choice has 2 hats.

Directions for the rest: Which answer choice would go inside the empty box at the bottom?

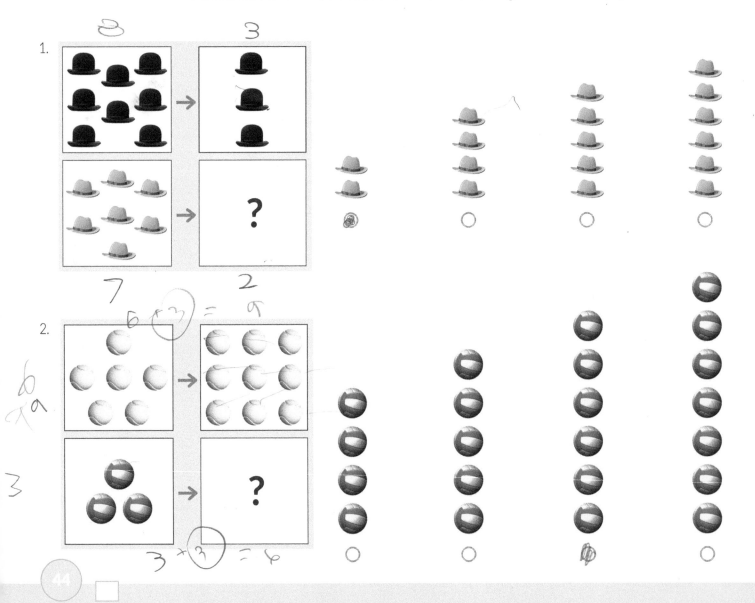

3.

1 + 4 = 5

+ 4 =

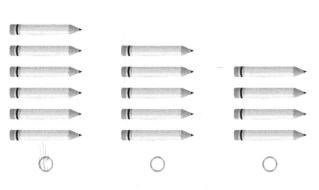

4.

9 - 4 = 5

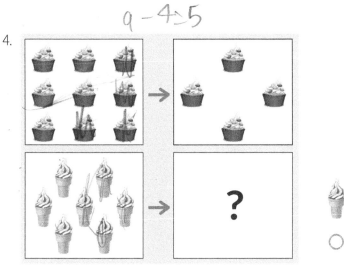

5.

5   5

6.

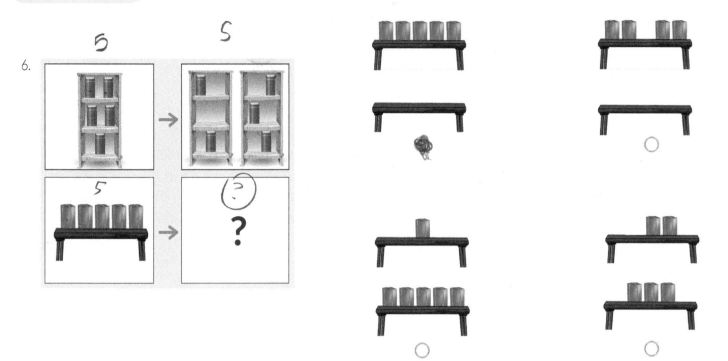

5

7.

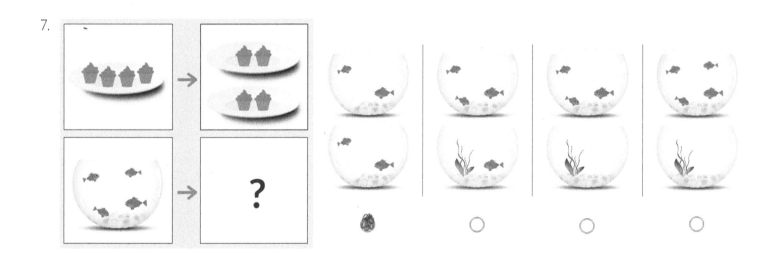

8.

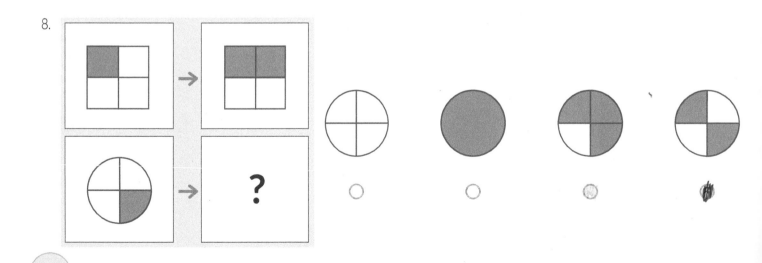

9.

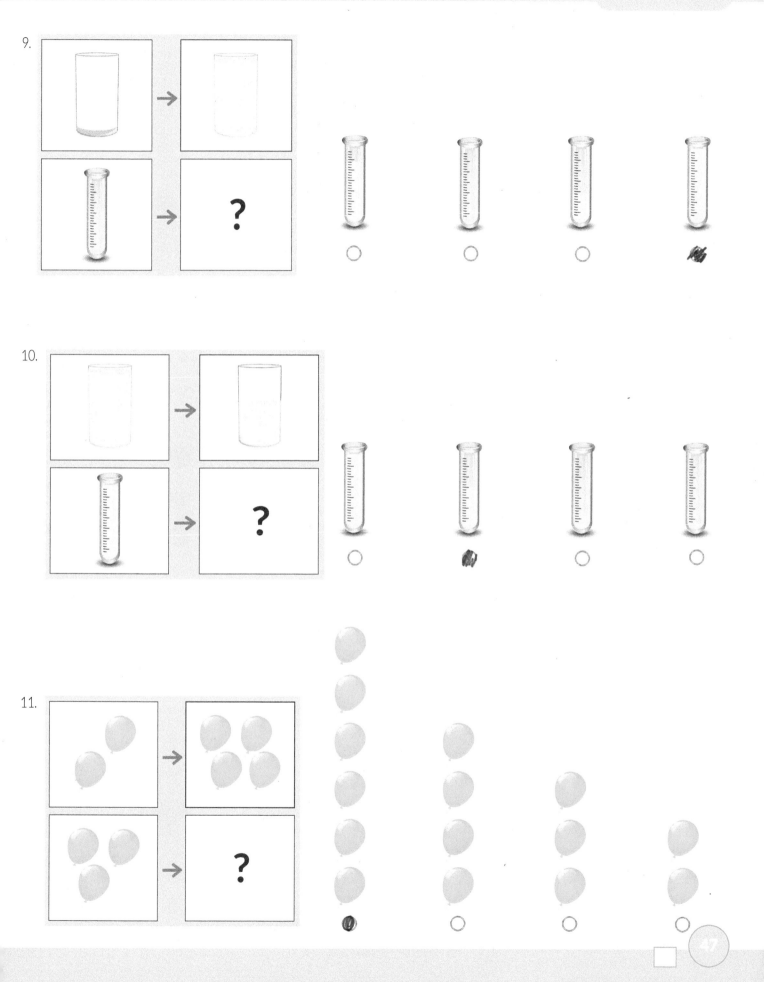

10.

11.

36   10 1D

12.

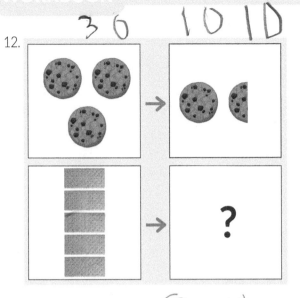

  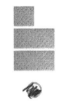

4 + ⑧ = MATH 2

13.

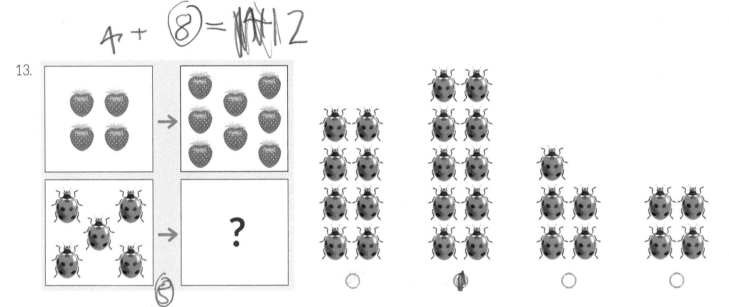

14.

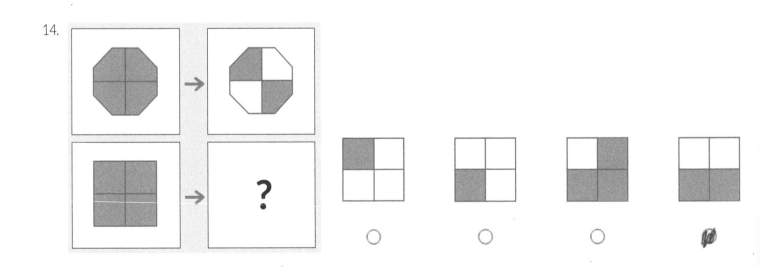

PRACTICE QUESTION SET INSTRUCTIONS

Pages 91-95 are the Directions and Answer Key for the Practice Question Set. These include question prompts.

Reading Directions: Tell your child to listen carefully (like a detective!), because you can read the directions to him/her only one time. (Test administrators often read directions only once.)

Test instructors will not let your child know if his/her answers are correct/incorrect. If you wish for the Practice Question Set to serve as a "practice test," then as your child completes the Practice Question Set, we suggest you do the same. Instead of saying if answers are correct/incorrect, you could say something like, "Nice work, let's try some more."

Navigation Figures: Assuming your child has completed the Workbook, then (s)he is familiar with the exercise format (navigating through pages with rows of questions). To make the test navigation easier for kids, some gifted tests use image markers in place of question numbers and in place of page numbers.

We include the "markers" so that your child can be familiar with them.

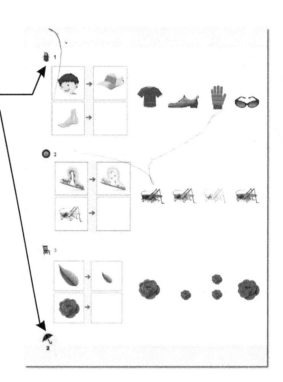

When your child needs to look at a new page, you would say, for example, "Find the page where there is an umbrella at the bottom." When your child needs to look at a question, you would say, for example, "Find the row where there is a bug."

These markers are listed on the Directions & Answer Key pages so that you can read them to your child.

The Practice Question Set is divided into three sections, to mirror the different "batteries" of the COGAT®: Verbal Section, Quantitative Section, and the Non-Verbal Section.

Time: Allow one minute per question, approximately.

Evaluation: The Practice Question Set is labeled by question type. After your child is done, on your own (without your child) go through the Set by question type, writing the number answered correctly in the space provided on the answer key. While these practice questions are not meant to be used in place of an official assessment, these will provide a general overview of strengths/weaknesses, as they pertain to test question type. For questions your child didn't answer correctly, go over the question and answer choices again with him/her. Compare the answer choices, specifically what makes the correct answer choice the right choice. Since gifted programs typically accept only top performers, we encourage additional practice.

We offer additional practice books as well as FREE questions in e-book format.
See page 96 and get your free e-book today!

1.

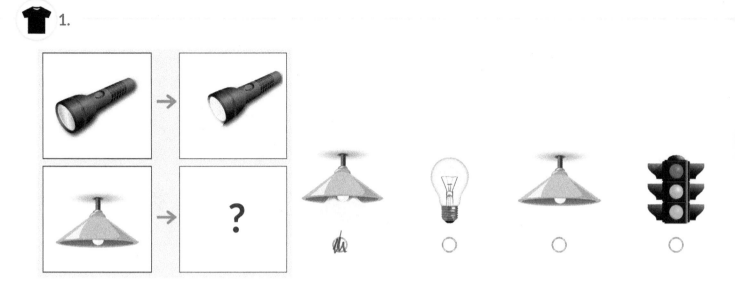

2.

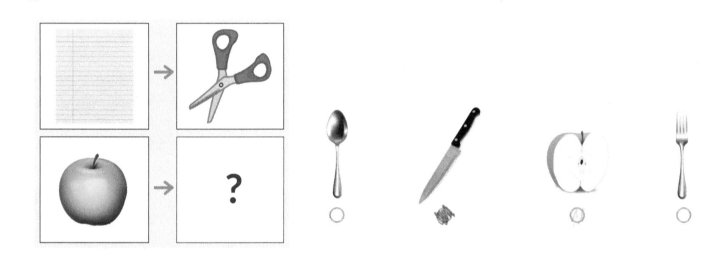

3.

4.

5.

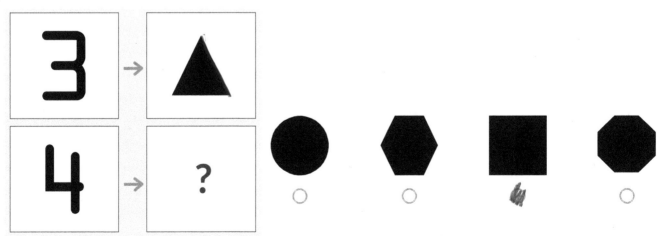

6.

7.

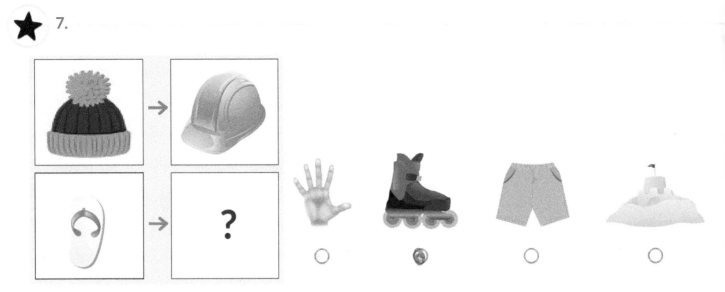

8.

9.

10.

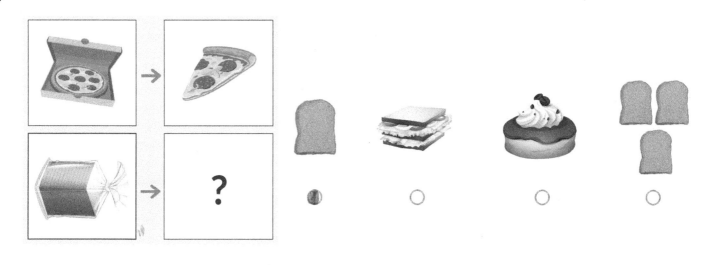

11.

12.

13.

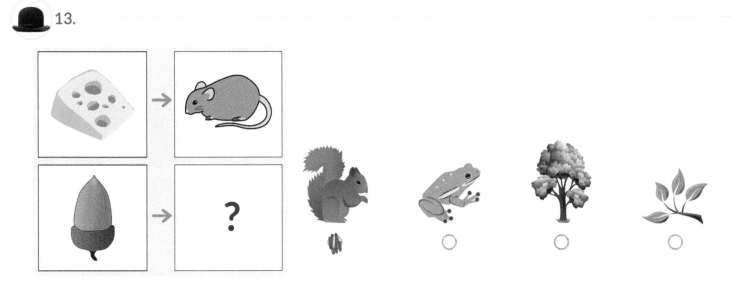

14.

15.

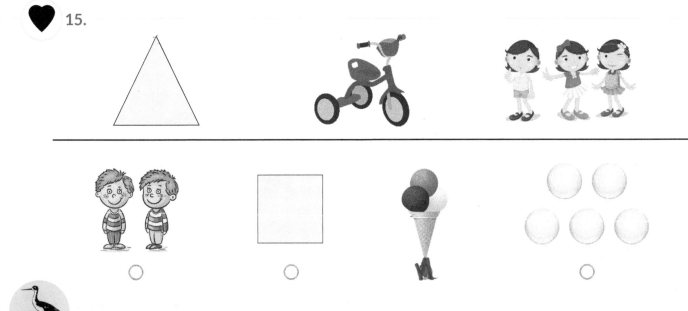

20.

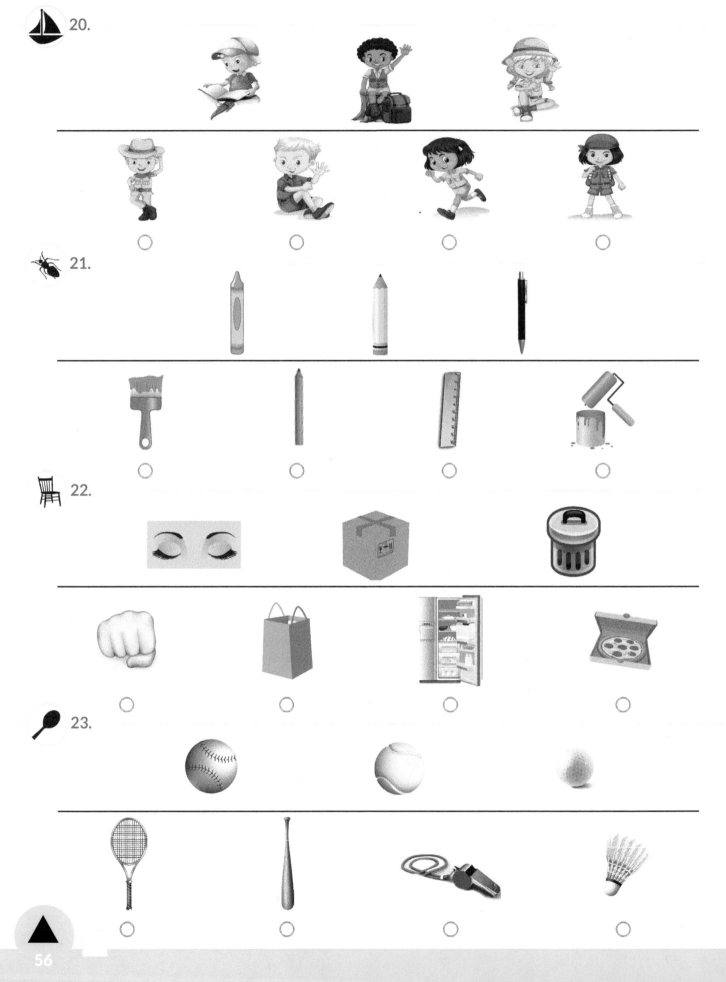

21.

22.

23.

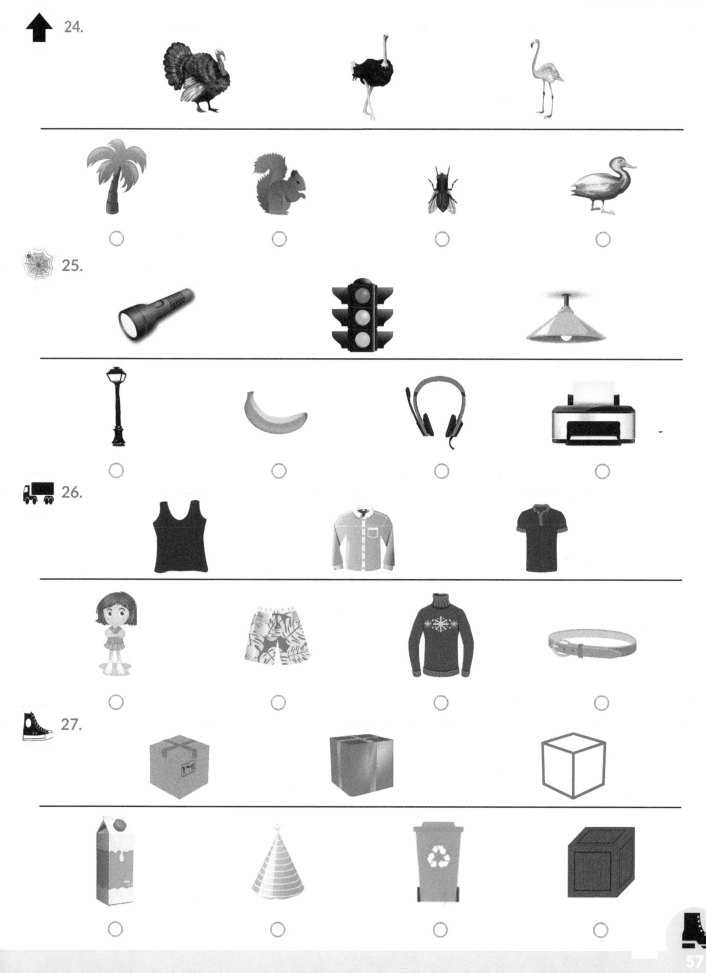

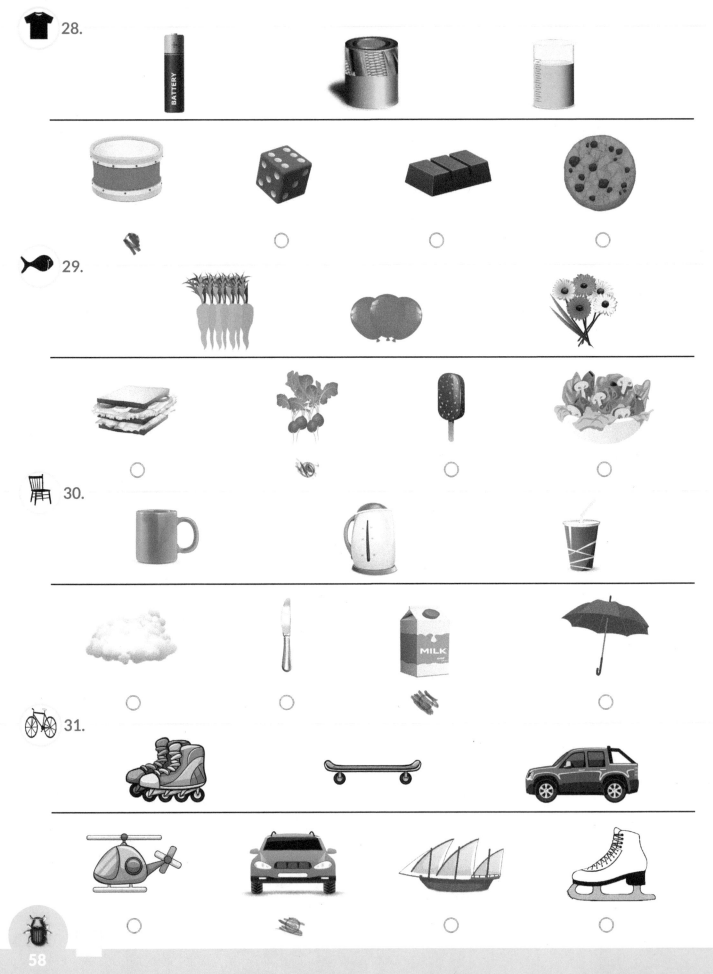

28.

29.

30.

31.

32.

○   ○   ○

 33.

○   ○   ○

34.

        ○   ○   ○

35.

○   ●   ○   ○

36.

○　　○　　○　　

 37.

　　○　　○　　○

38.

○　　○　　○　　○

 39.

 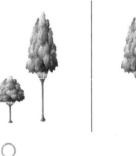 

○　　○　　○　　○

40.

○   ○   ○   ○

 41.

○   ○   ○   ○

42.

○   ○   ○   ○

43.

○   ○   ○   ○

44.

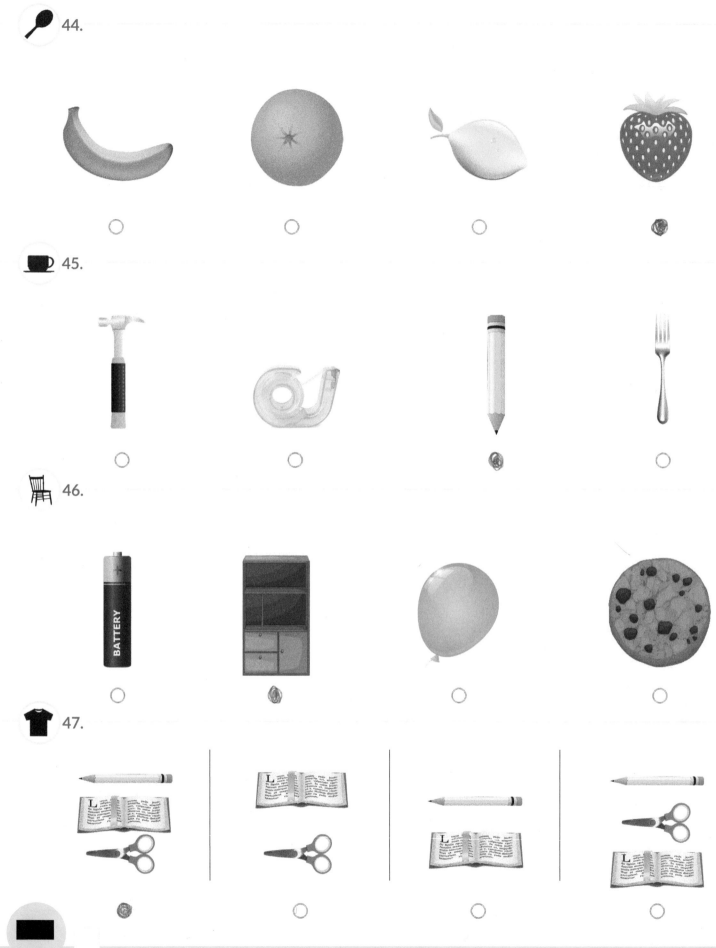

45.

46.

47.

★ 48.

↑ 49.

🔑 50.

🪲 51.

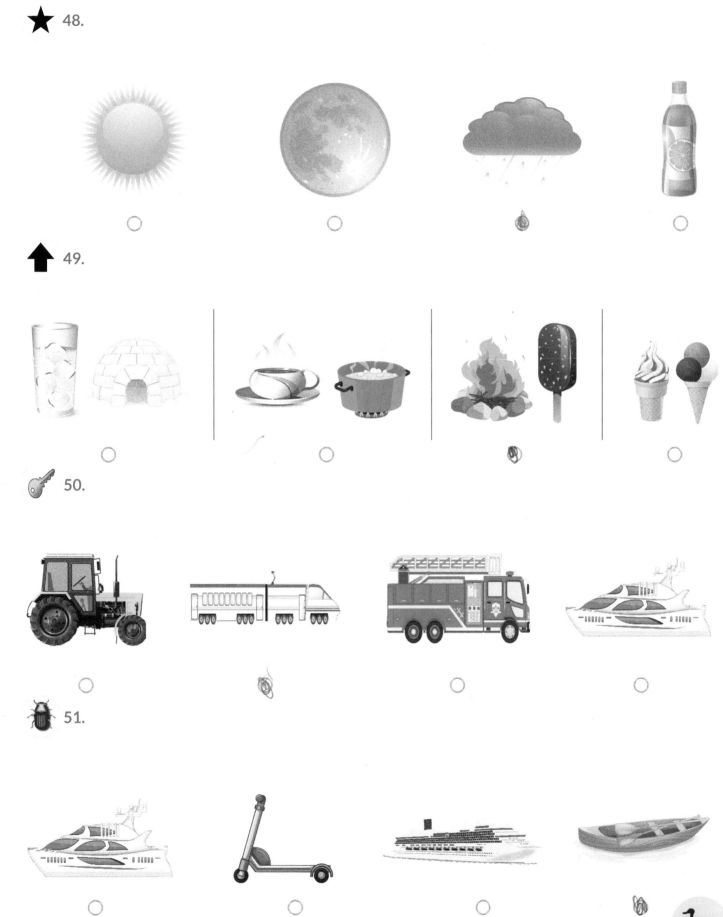

52. 9 9 + 2 = 10 7

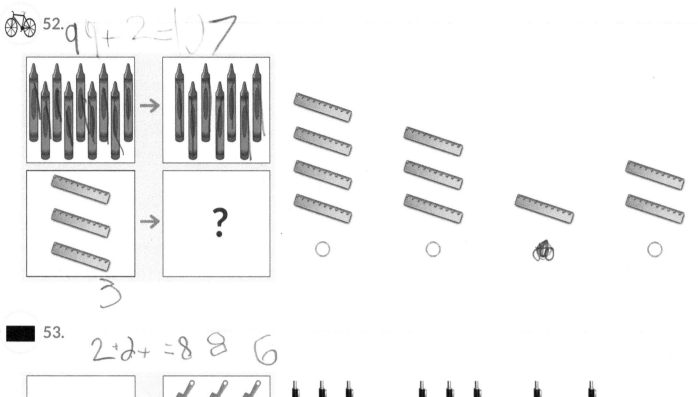

3

53. 2 + 2 + = 8 8 6

9

9 = 2 + 3

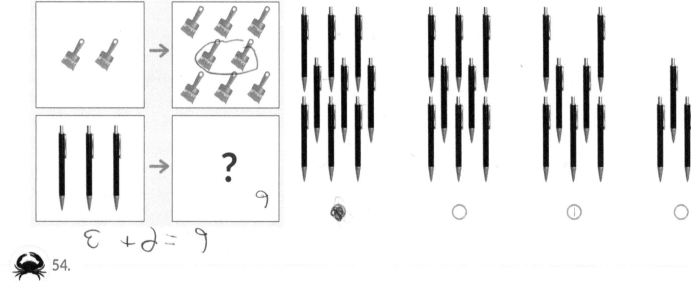

54.

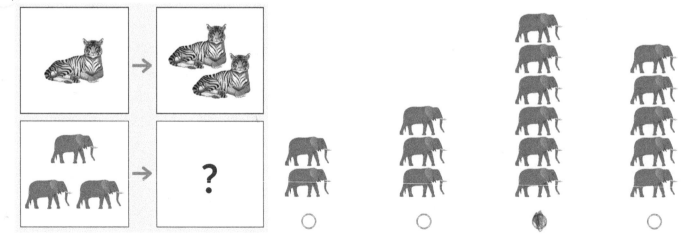

55.

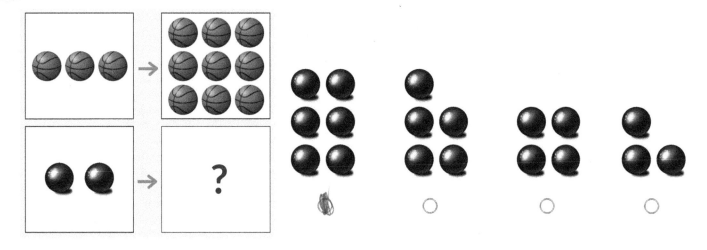

56.

57. 8

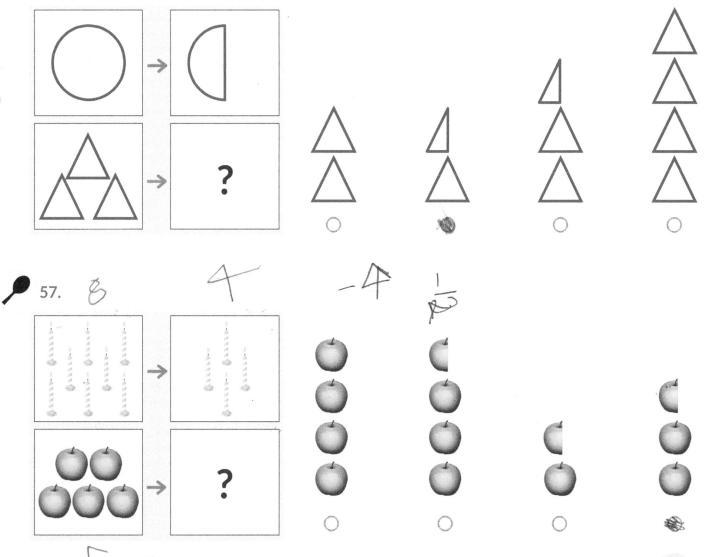

5-

58.

10

5

9-5 =4

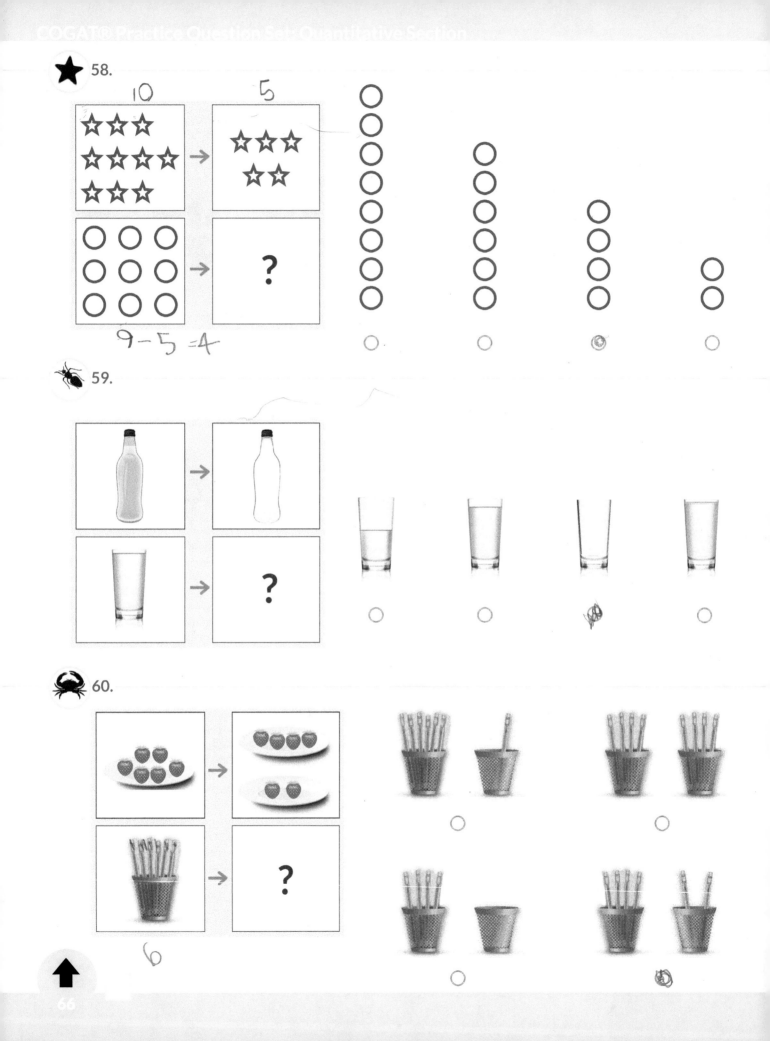

59.

60.

6

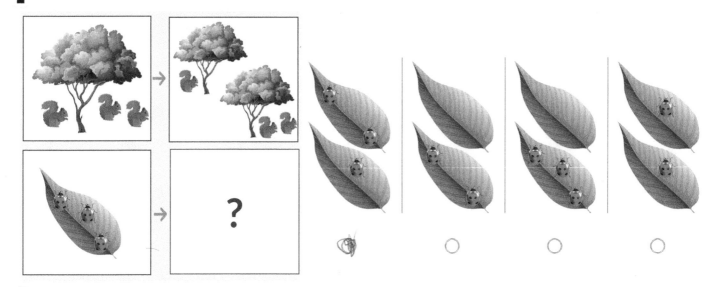

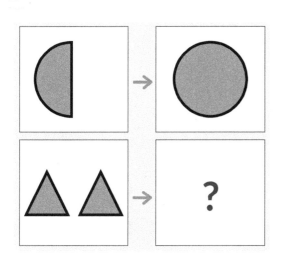

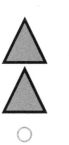

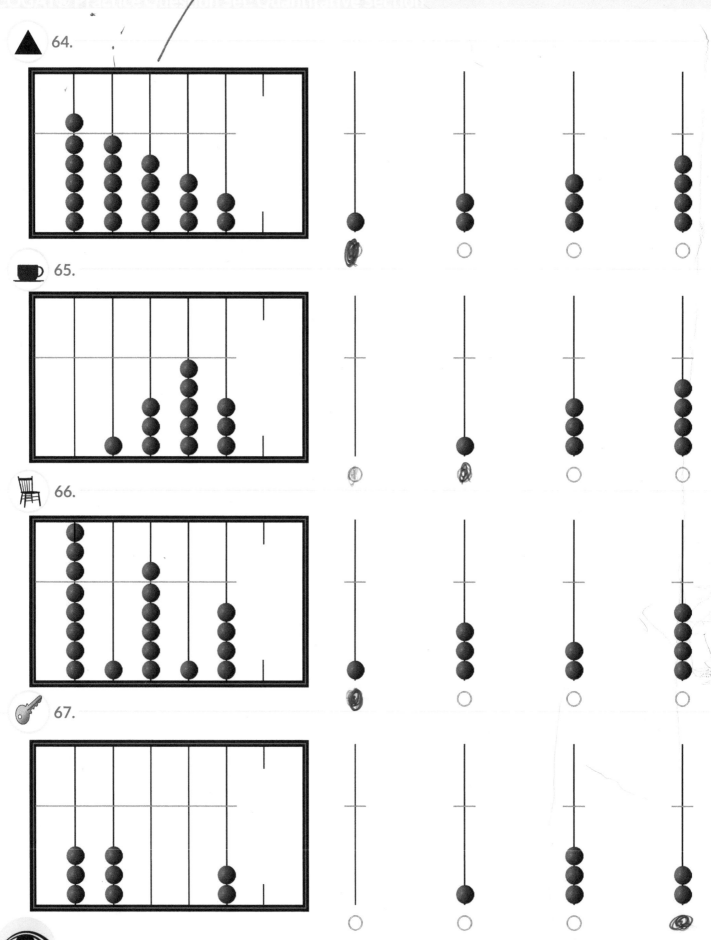

64.

65.

66.

67.

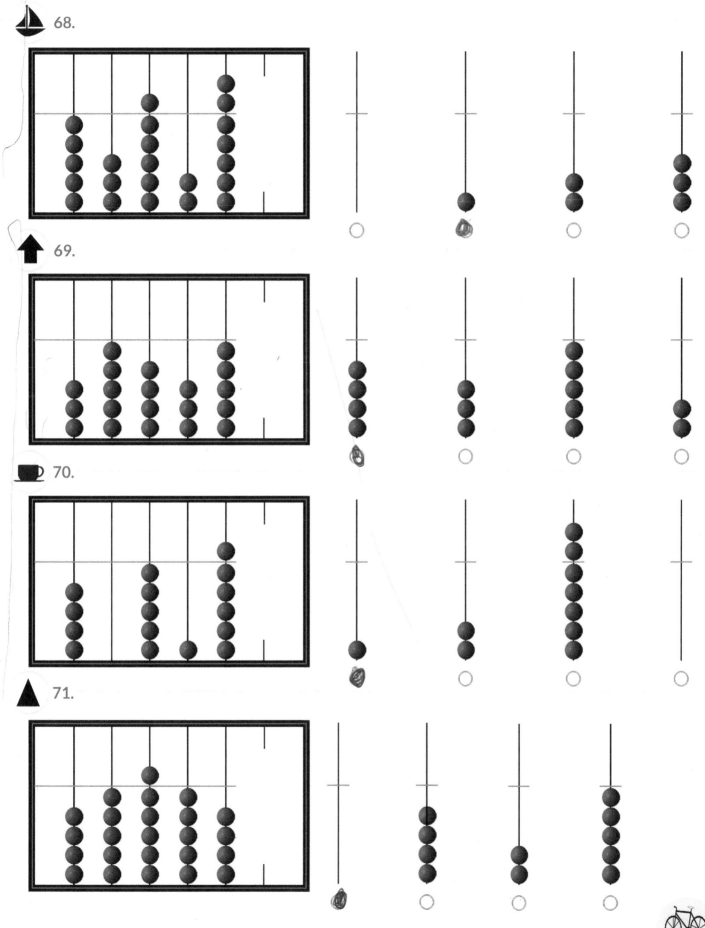

68.

69.

70.

71.

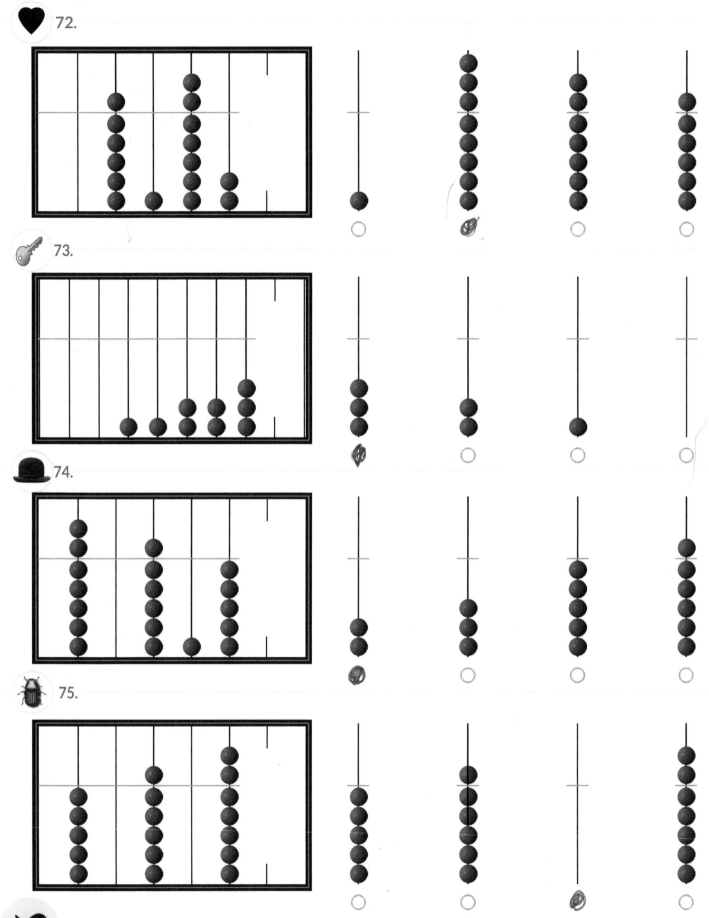

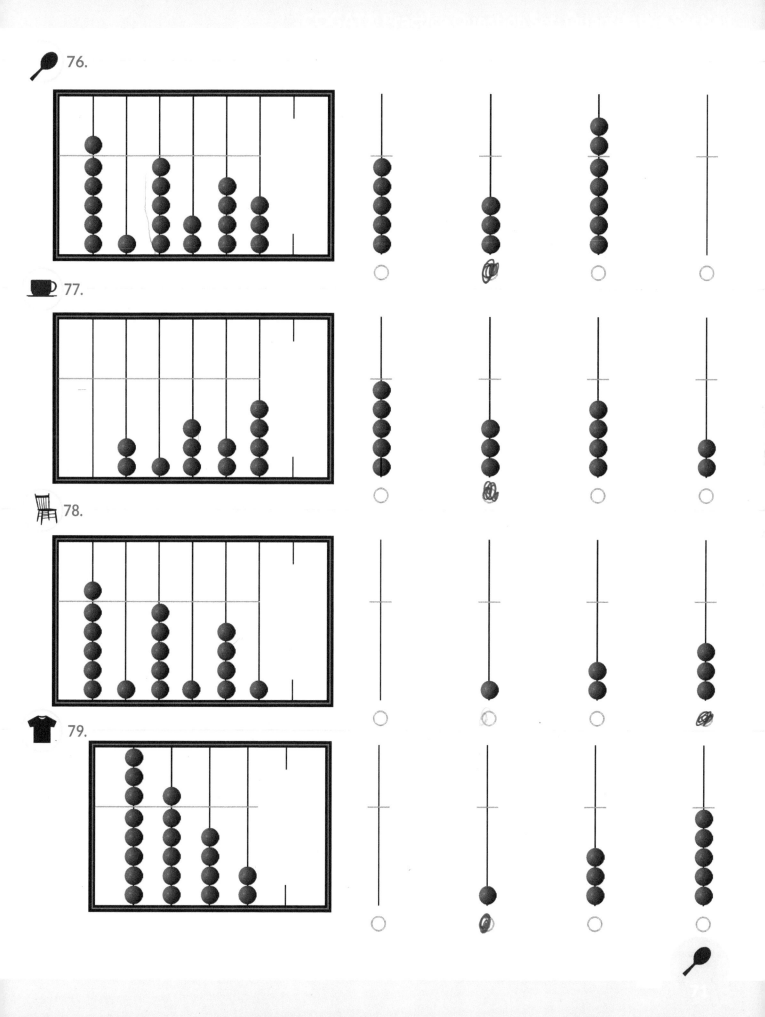

76.

77.

78.

79.

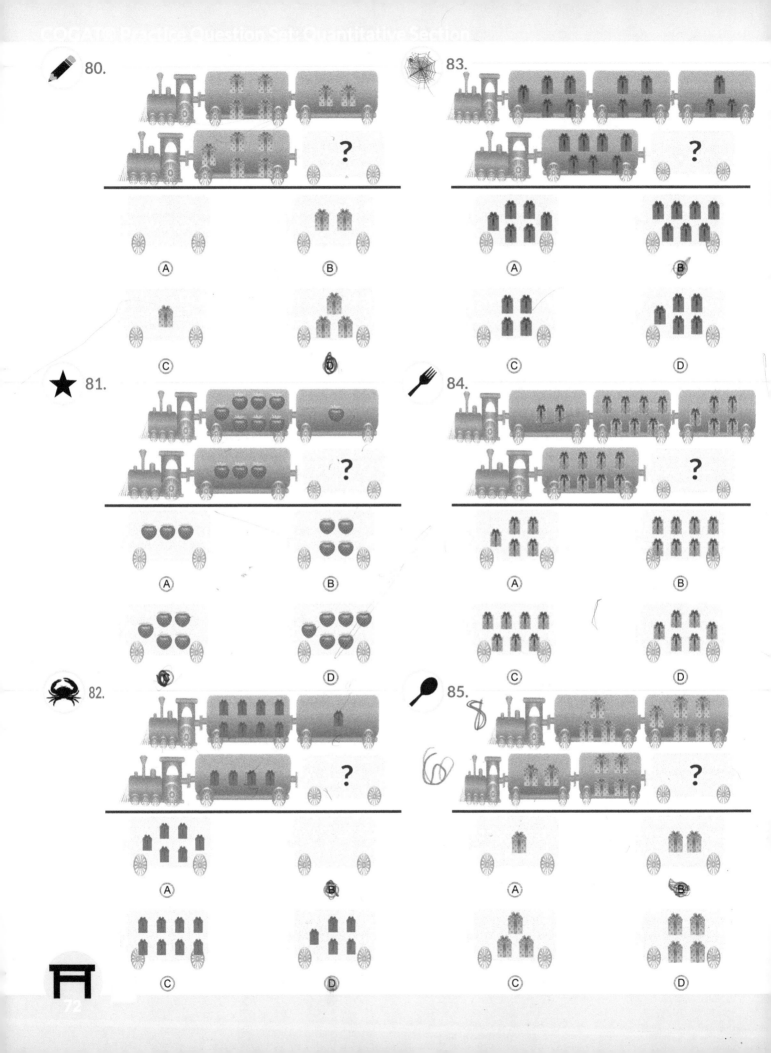

80.

A B C D

81.

A B C D

82.

A B C D

83.

A B C D

84.

A B C D

85.

A B C D

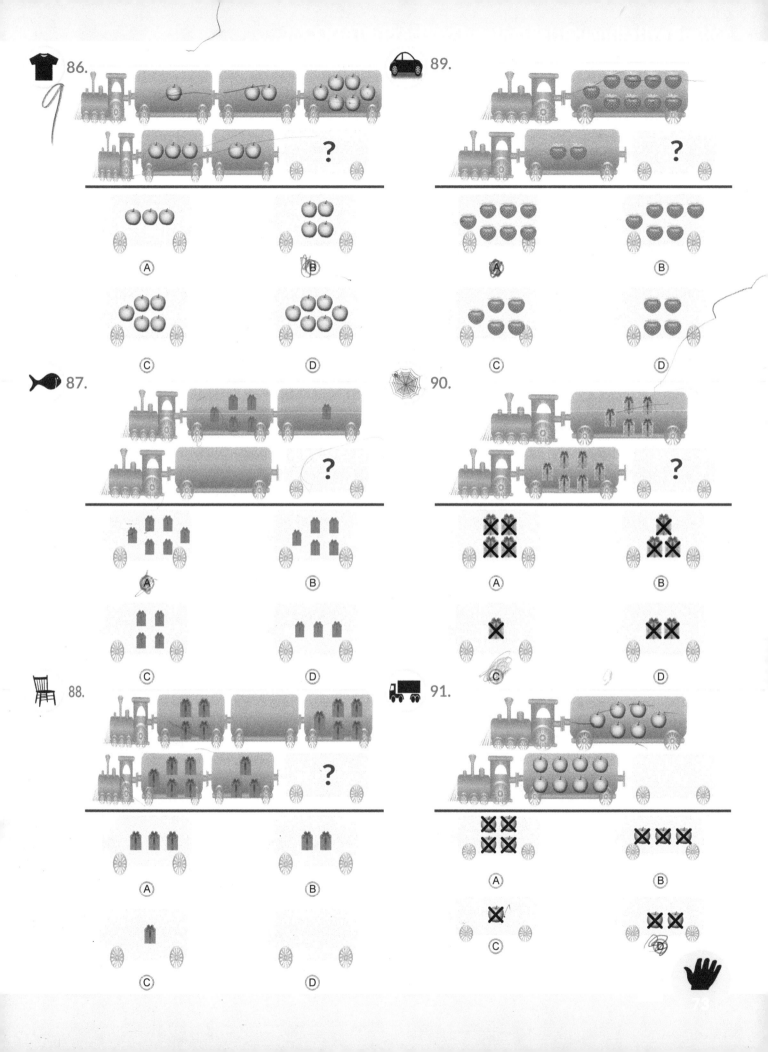

86.

A

B

C

D

87.

A

B

C

D

88.

A

B

C

D

89.

A

B

C

D

90.

A

B

C

D

91.

A

B

C

D

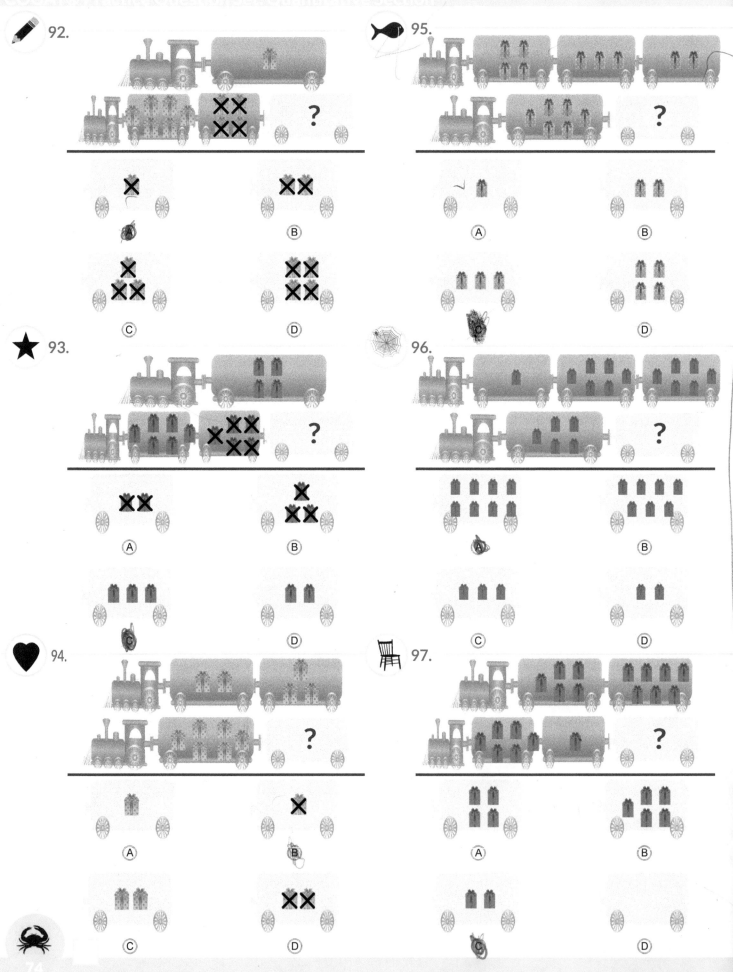

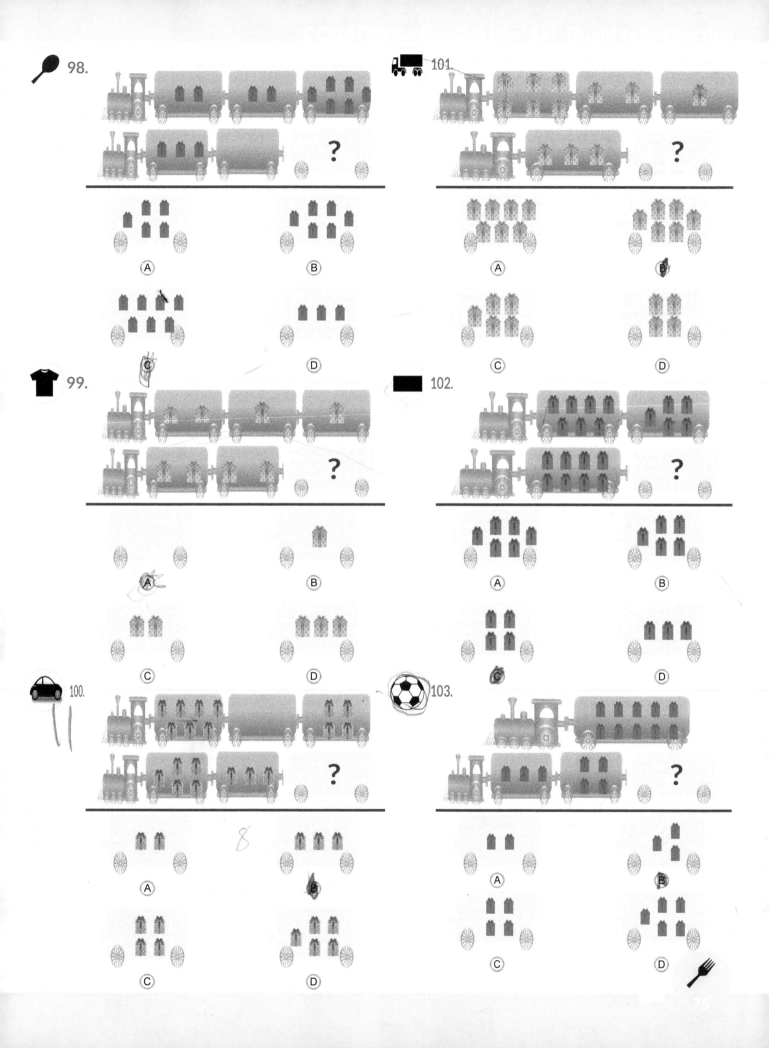

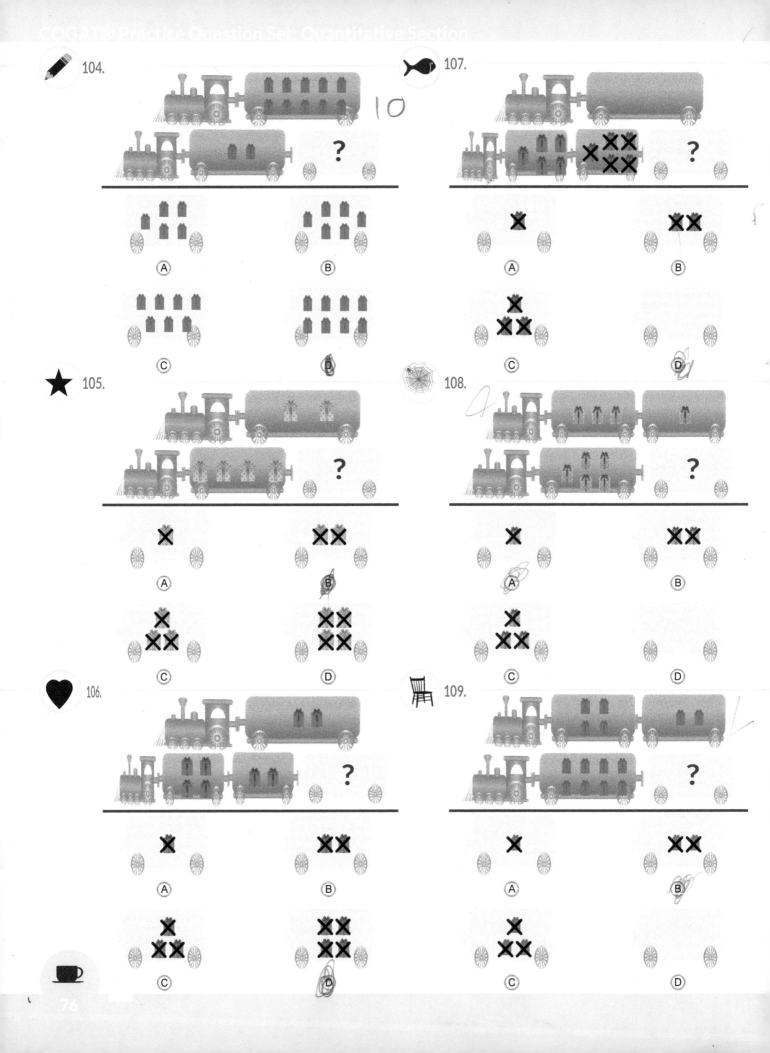

104.

107.

A

B

C

D

105.

108.

A

B

C

D

106.

109.

A

B

C

D

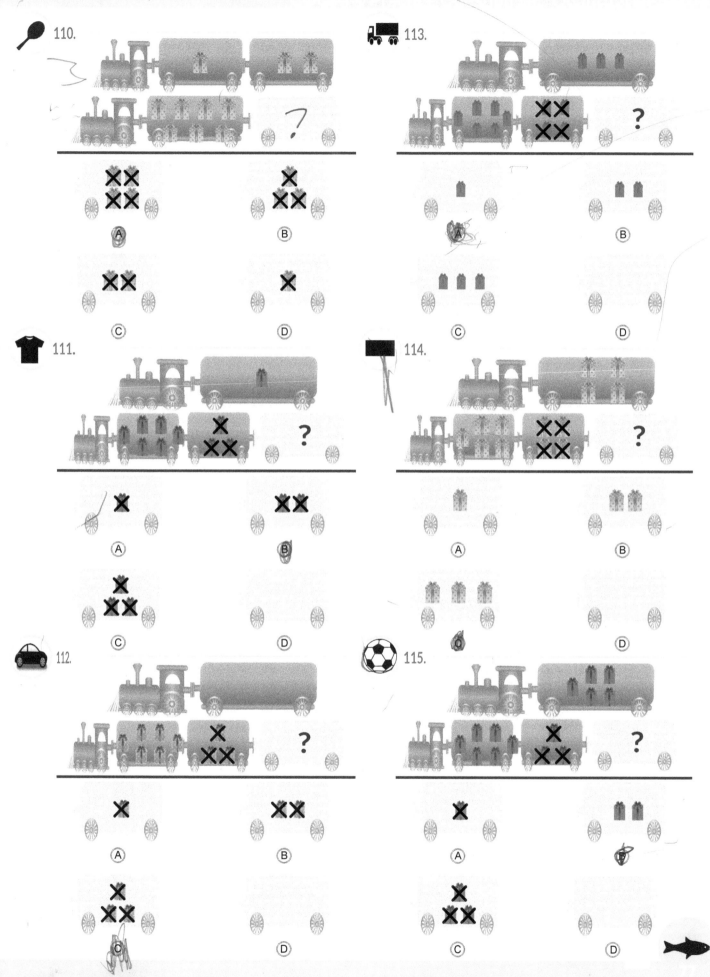

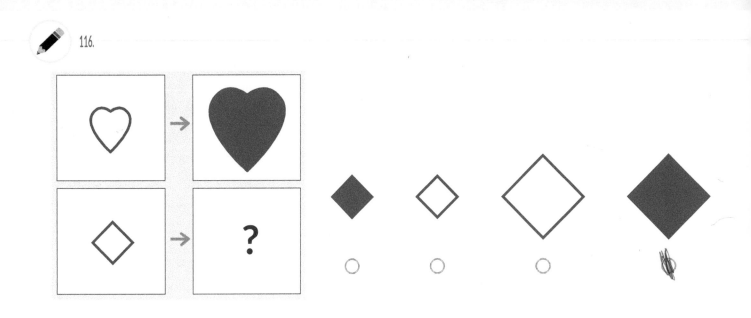

116.

117.

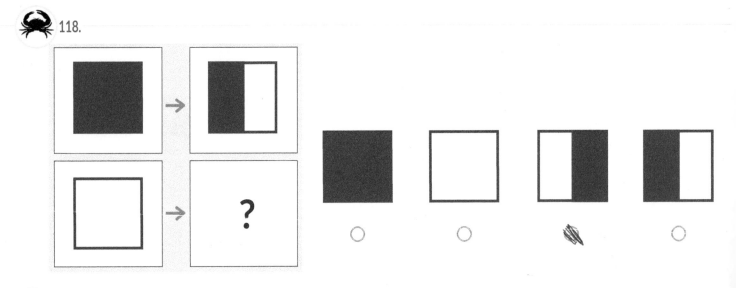

118.

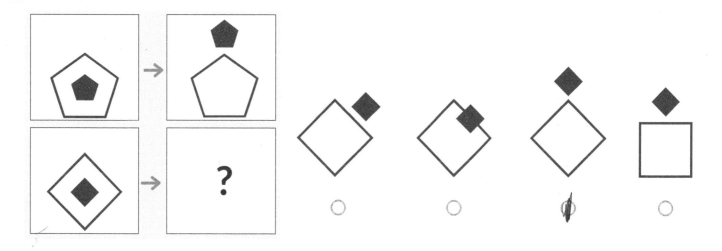

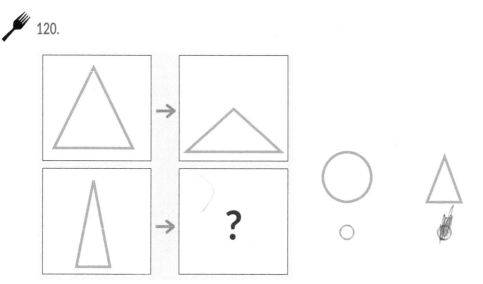

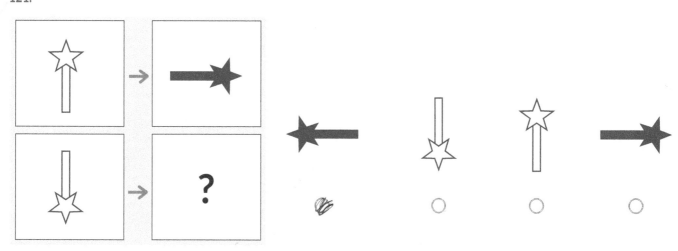

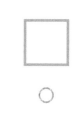

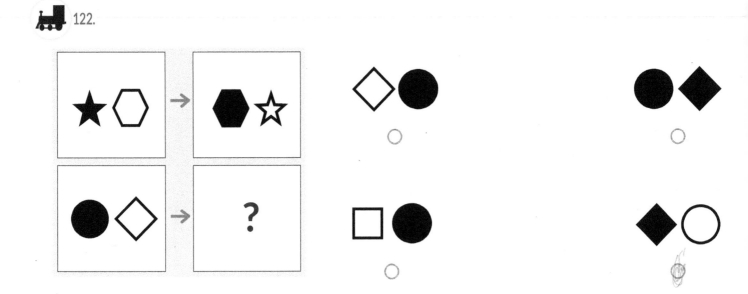

122.

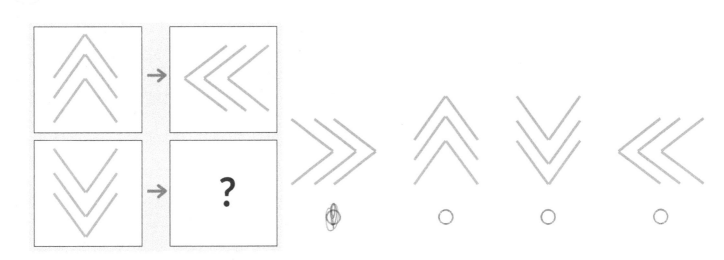

123.

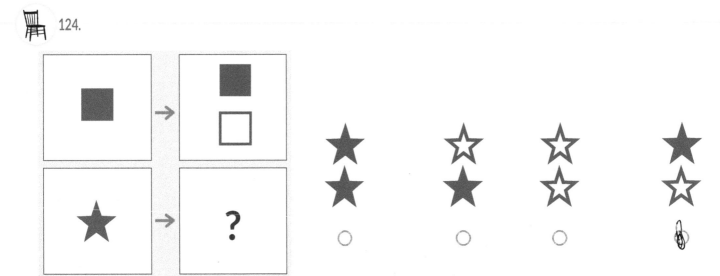

124.

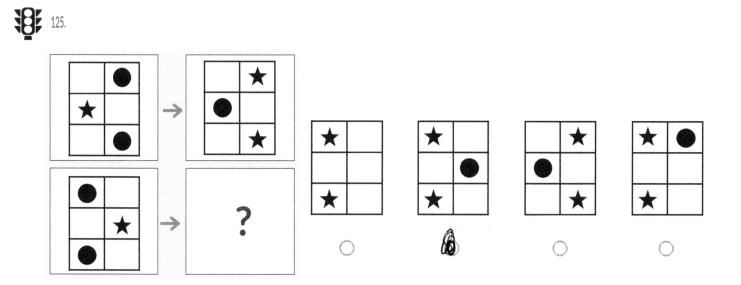

125.

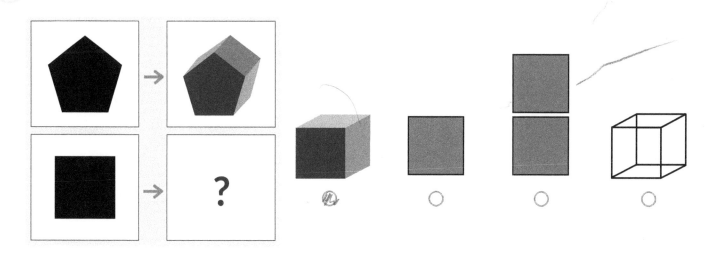

126.

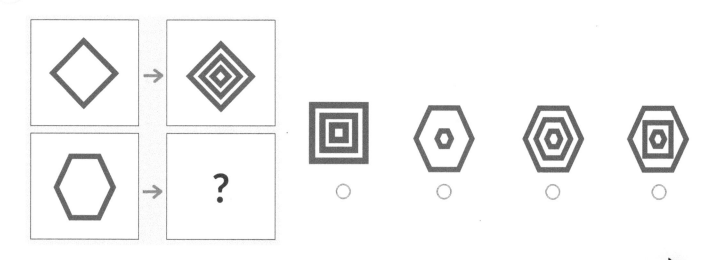

127.

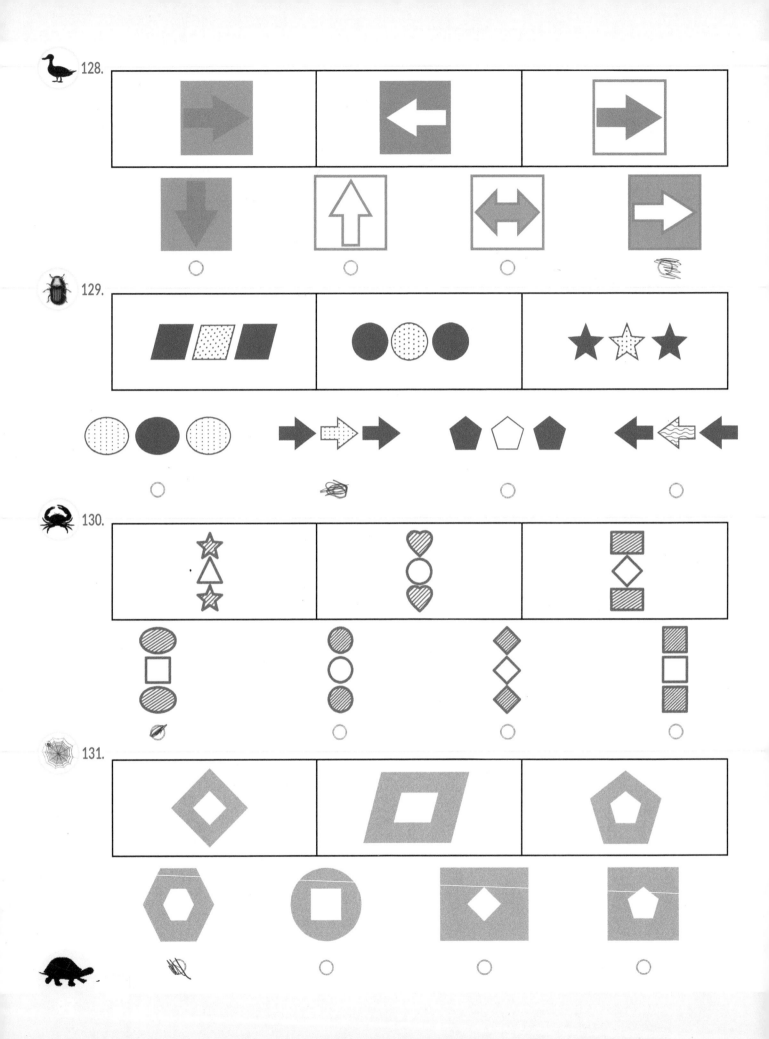

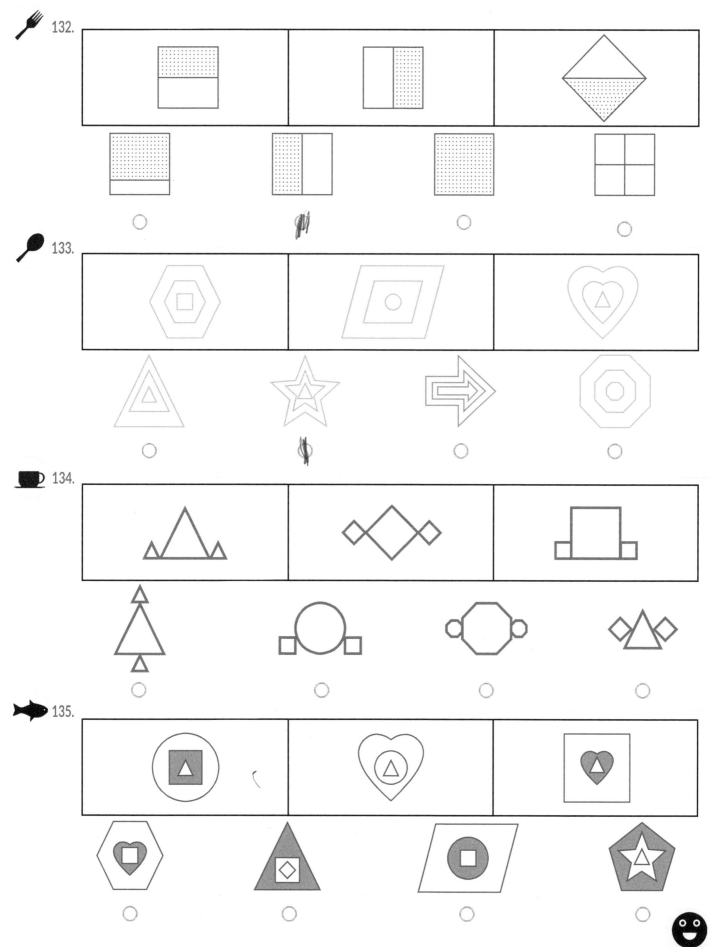

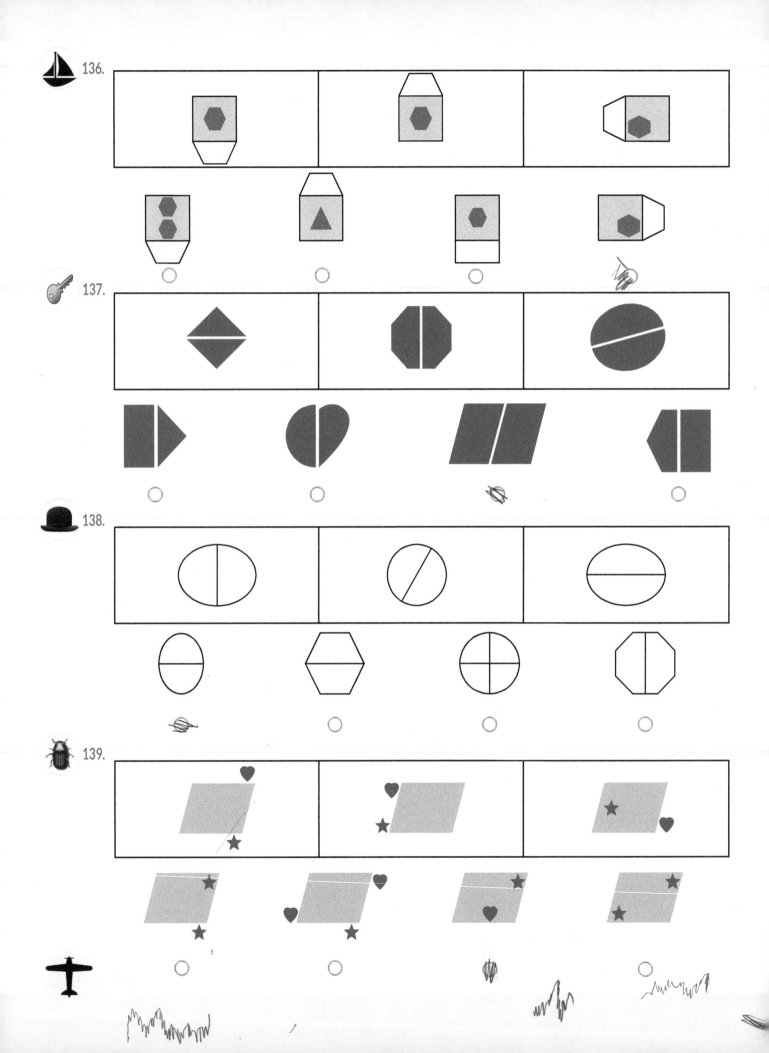

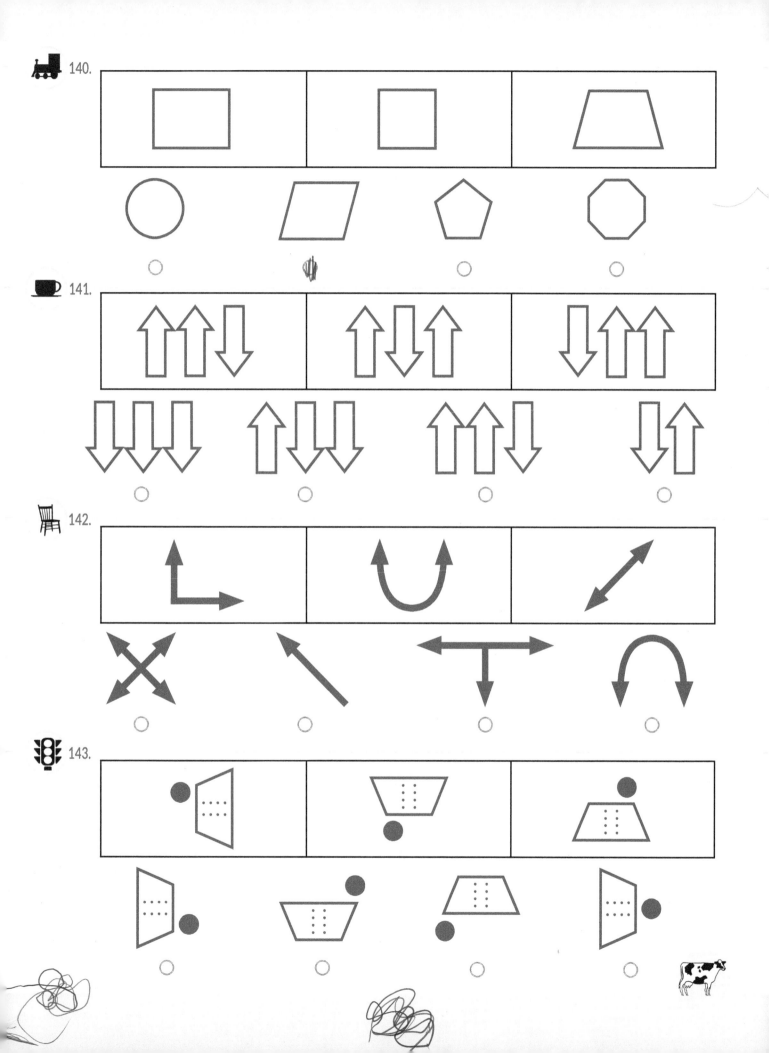

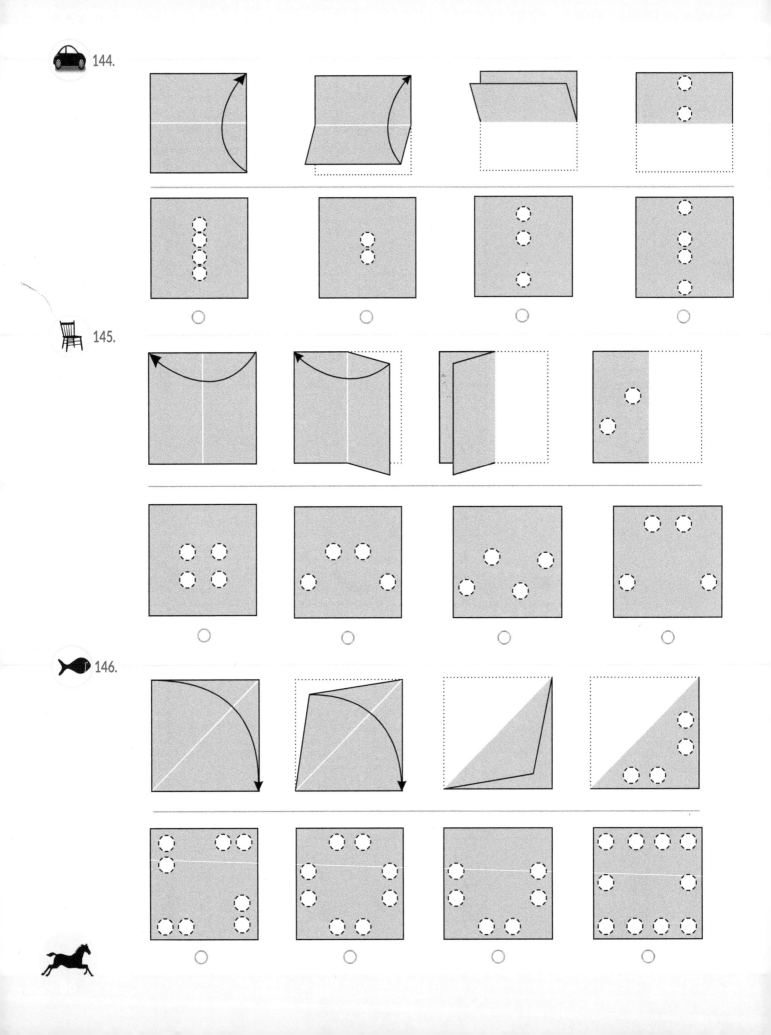

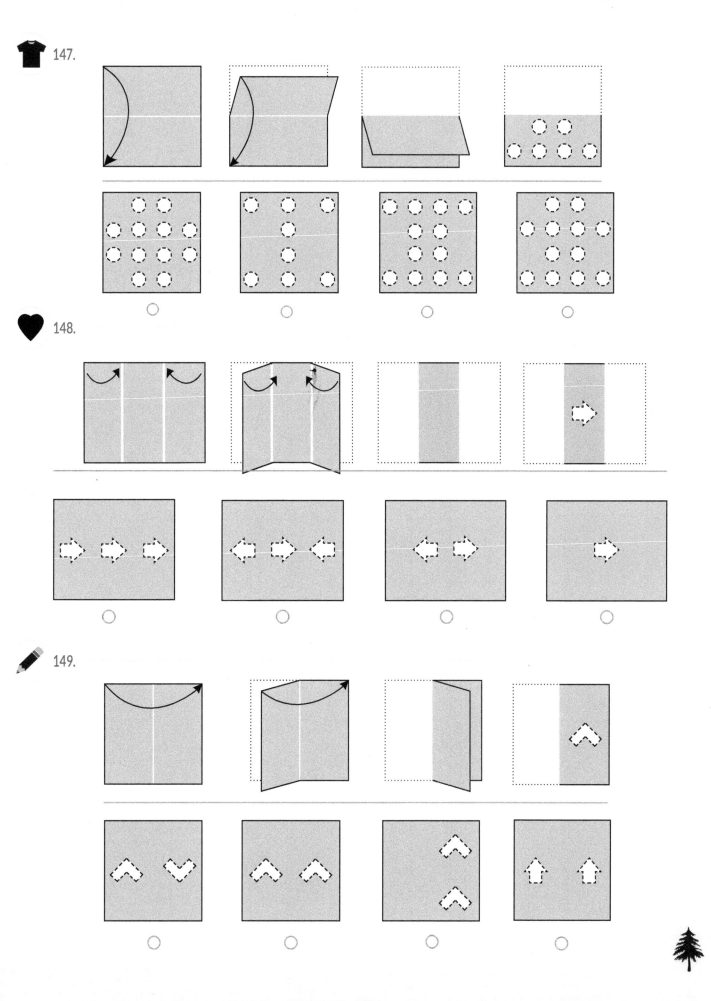

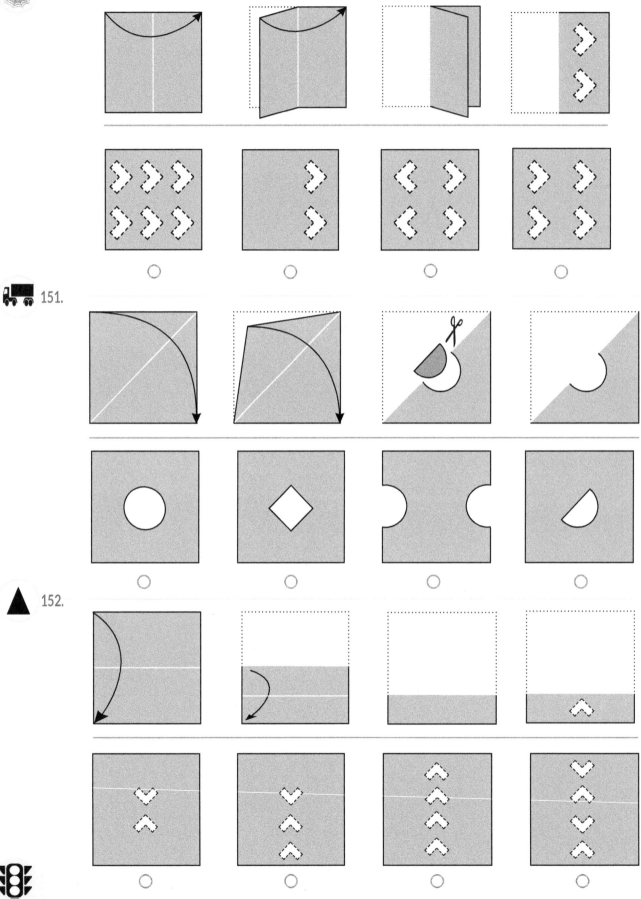

150.

151.

152.

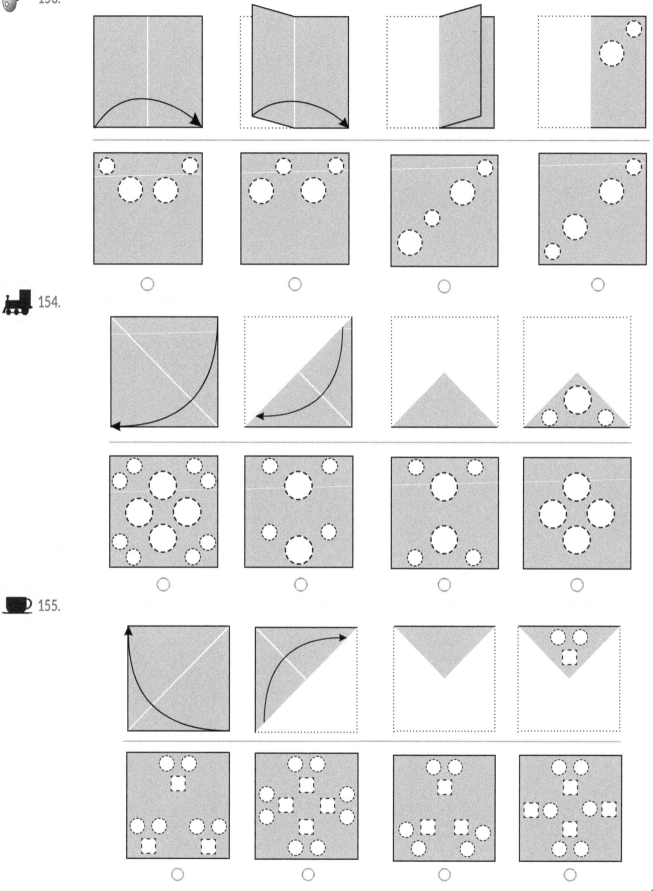

ANSWER KEY FOR WORKBOOK (p.10-48)

Skill Builders (Pictures)
1. D (farm animals)
2. C (have lenses/used to see things more closely)
3. D (orange)
4. A (buildings where people could live)
5. B (fruit)
6. D (warm weather clothes)
7. A (kitchen appliances/used to heat food)
8. D (3 items)
9. C (animal homes)
10. B (items used to write)
11. D (objects hold paper together)
12. D (places with water)
13. B (fruits that grow on trees)
14. A (vegetables)

Skill Builders (Shapes)
1. D (diagonal lines go upper left to bottom right)
2. C (2 boxes filled in and/or top box filled in)
3. B (shapes with no corners)
4. C (hexagon in middle)
5. C (3 shapes)
6. C (2 pointed arrows)
7. B (shapes decrease in size left to right)
8. C (4-sided shapes)
9. B (curvy lines upper left to lower right)
10. D (6-sided shapes)
11. D (3-D shapes)
12. A (shapes get bigger)
13. C (arrows pointing different directions; 2 down, 1 up)
14. B (shapes that aren't rounded)
15. D (1/2 filled)

Picture Analogies
1. B
2. D (object seen in sky > when you would see it)
3. A (water on > water off)
4. A (fruit slice > whole fruit)
5. D (food or drink > item used to consume it)
6. B (closed > open)
7. C (type of weather > activity typical to this weather)
8. C (one arm up > both arms out to the side)
9. A (ball > sports equipment used to hit ball)
10. D (animal > animal's enclosed home)

Figure Analogies
1. C (flips -or- rotates clockwise)
2. B (rotates 90 degrees clockwise)
3. D (small middle shape gets bigger)
4. A (colors reverse)
5. B (large and small shapes switch position)
6. C (same)

Picture Classification
1. D
2. B (homes)
3. C (tell time)
4. C (used to go up/down to a different level)
5. A (2-D/flat shape)
6. C (toy animals)
7. D (pairs)
8. C (cold objects)
9. B (fruit)
10. A (sweets)
11. D (worn on feet)
12. D (tools)
13. C (community helpers)
14. B (have stripes/striped fish)

Figure Classification
1. C (white line going from lower left to upper right)
2. B (four lines inside shape)
3. C (2 sections (half) of square filled in)
4. B (shape filled in - shape with dots - shape filled in)
5. B (4 shapes)
6. A (white shape with dark shape in middle)
7. B (2 of same smaller shape across from each other)
8. D (hexagon and triangle filled in)

Can You Find It? (Sentence Completion)
1. A	4. D	7. A	10. A	13. C	16. D	19. C
2. B	5. A	8. B	11. C	14. D	17. B	
3. C	6. C	9. D	12. B	15. A	18. A	

Paper Folding Puzzles
1. C	5. C	9. B	13. D	17. C	21. C
2. D	6. D	10. A	14. A	18. D	
3. A	7. C	11. B	15. D	19. D	
4. C	8. C	12. C	16. A	20. B	

Number Series (Abacus Activity)
1. B
2. A (every other rod has 0)
3. B (6-6-7-7-4-4)
4. C (rods 1,3,5 & rods 2,4,6 increase by 1)
5. D (5-3-1-0-1-3)
6. A (6-2-4-6-2-4)
7. C (4-4-3-3-2-2-1-1)
8. D (each rod +2)
9. C (rods 1,3,5,7 & rods 2,4,6 increase by 1)
10. A (1-1-4-1-1-4)

Number Puzzles (Train Activity)
1. B	2. C	3. C	4. A	5. C	6. D	7. D
8. B	9. C	10. C	11. A	12. A		

Number Analogies
1. A	2. C	3. A	4. C

5. B
6. D (5 objects (books/presents) > same 5 objects split between two shelves, then, two tables)
7. A (same logic as #6, this time with 4 objects)
8. D (1 section filled > 2 sections filled)
9. D (empty > full)
10. B (full > half full)
11. A (doubles)
12. C (halved)
13. B (doubles)
14. D (whole filled > half filled; 4 filled > 2 filled)

COGAT® QUESTION TYPE 4: NUMBER ANALOGIES, CONTINUED (QUANTITATIVE SECTION)

"Find the row where there is a(n) _____."	Question Number	Answer	Child's Answer
(p. 65) *"Find the page where there is a flower at the bottom."*			
Car	55	A (multiply by 3)	
Fork	56	B (half)	
Spoon	57	D (half)	
(p. 66) *"Find the page where there is a black arrow at the bottom."*			
Star	58	C (-5)	
Bug	59	C (full > empty)	
Crab	60	D (6 items>6 split, 4 and 2)	
(p. 67) *"Find the page where there is a shirt at the bottom."*			
Stoplight	61	A (3 things, 3 split, 1 and 2)	
Fork	62	C	
Eye	63	B (doubles)	

Number Analogies Questions Answered Correctly: _____ out of 12

COGAT® QUESTION TYPE 5: NUMBER SERIES - ABACUS (QUANTITATIVE SECTION)

Directions for all Number Series questions: Here's an abacus. The "circles" on the abacus are beads. These beads are on rods. The beads on the first rods have made a pattern. Look at the last rod on the abacus. The beads on this rod are missing. Next to the abacus are four rods. These are the answer choices. Choose which rod would go in the place of the last rod in order to complete the pattern.

"Find the row where there is a(n) _____."	Question Number	Answer	Child's Answer
(p. 68) *"Find the page where there is an eye at the bottom."*			
Triangle	64	A	
Cup	65	B (0-1-3-5-3-1)	
Chair	66	A (every other rod as 1 bead)	
Key	67	D (3-3-0-0-2-2)	
(p. 69) *"Find the page where there is a bike at the bottom."*			
Boat	68	B (rods 1,3,5 increas 1; 2,4,6 decrease by 1)	
Arrow	69	A (3-5-4-3-5-4)	
Cup	70	B (rods 1,3,5 increas 1; 2,4,6 increase by 1)	
Triangle	71	D (4-5-6-5-4-5; 5 ds always follow 4 beads)	
(p. 70) *"Find the page where there is a fish at the bottom."*			
Heart	72	B (rods 1,3,5 increas y 1; 2,4,6 increase by 1)	
Key	73	A (0-0-1-1-2-2-3-	
Hat	74	A (rods 1,3,5 decrea by 1; 2,4,6 increase by 1)	
Bug	75	C (every other rod as 0 beads)	
(p. 71) *"Find the page where there is a spoon at the bottom."*			
Spoon	76	B (rods 1,3,5 decrea e by 1; 2,4,6 increase by 1)	
Cup	77	B (rods 1,3,5,7 increase by 1; 2,4,6 increase by 1)	
Chair	78	D (rods 1,3,5,7 decrease by 1; 2,4,6 = 1)	
Shirt	79	A (each rod decreases by 2)	

Number Series Questions Answered Correctly: _____ out of 16

COGAT® QUESTION TYPE 6: MATH PUZZLES - TRAINS (QUANTITATIVE SECTION)

Directions for all Math Puzzles questions: Look at the trains on the top and bottom. They have things inside. These two trains must have the same number of things. You need to put a train car in place of the train car that has a question mark so that the second train has the same number of things as the other train. Which train car should you choose so that the second train has the same number of things as the first train?

"Find the row with a(n) _____."	Question Number	Answer	Child's Answer
(p. 72) *"Find the page with a table at the bottom."*			
Pencil	80	C	
Star	81	C	
Crab	82	D	
Web	83	D	
Fork	84	D	
Spoon	85	B	

COGAT® QUESTION TYPE 6: MATH PUZZLES (TRAIN), CONTINUED (QUANTITATIVE SECTION)

"Find the row with a(n) ____."	Question Number	Answer	Child's Answer	"Find the row with a(n) ____."	Question Number	Answer	Child's Answer
(p. 73) *"Find the page with a hand at the bottom."*				(p. 76) *"Find the page with a cup at the bottom."*			
Shirt	86	B		Pencil	104	D	
Fish	87	A		Star	105	B	
Chair	88	C		Heart	106	D	
Car	89	A		Fish	107	D	
Web	90	C		Web	108	A	
Truck	91	D		Chair	109	B	
(p. 74) *"Find the page with a crab at the bottom."*				(p. 77) *"Find the page with a fish at the bottom."*			
Pencil	92	A		Spoon	110	A	
Star	93	C		Shirt	111	B	
Heart	94	B		Car	112	C	
Fish	95	C		Truck	113	A	
Web	96	A		Rectangle	114	C	
Chair	97	B		Ball	115	B	
(p. 75) *"Find the page with a fork at the bottom."*							
Spoon	98	C					
Shirt	99	A					
Car	100	B					
Truck	101	B					
Rectangle	102	C					
Ball	103	B					

Math Puzzles Questions Answered Correctly:
_____ out of 36

COGAT® QUESTION TYPE 7: FIGURE ANALOGIES (NON-VERBAL SECTION)

Directions for all Figure Analogy questions: Look at these boxes that are on top. The pictures that are inside belong together in some way. Then, look at these boxes that are on the bottom. One of these boxes on the bottom is empty. Look next to the boxes. There is a row of pictures. Which one would go together with this picture that is in the bottom box like these pictures that are in the top boxes?

"Find the row where there is a(n) ____."	Question Number	Answer	Child's Answer
(p. 78) *"Find the page where there is an ant at the bottom."*			
Pencil	116	D (gets larger, becomes dark)	
Stoplight	117	D (shapes reverse colors)	
Crab	118	C (left half of shape remains same color as in first box, right half turns opposite color)	
(p. 79) *"Find the page where there is a hat at the bottom."*			
Cup	119	C (middle shape moves above larger shape)	
Fork	120	B (triangles)	
Spoon	121	A (rotates clockwise, gets dark)	
(p. 80) *"Find the page where there is a wheel at the bottom."*			
Train	122	D (flips, becomes opposite color)	
Cup	123	A (rotates counterclockwise)	
Chair	124	D (white version of shape added underneath)	
(p. 81) *"Find the page where there is a fish at the bottom."*			
Stoplight	125	B (stars become circles; circles become stars)	
Boat	126	A (shape > 3D gray version of shape)	
House	127	C (shape > +2 smaller shapes added inside)	

Figure Analogy Questions Answered Correctly: _____ out of 12

COGAT® QUESTION TYPE 8: FIGURE CLASSIFICATION (NON-VERBAL SECTION)

Directions for all Figure Classification questions: Look at the top row of pictures. These pictures are alike in a certain way. Then, look at the pictures that are on the bottom row. Which picture that is in the bottom row would go best with the pictures that are in the top row?

"Find the row where there is a(n) _____."	Question Number	Answer	Child's Answer
(p. 82) *"Find the page where there is a turtle at the bottom."*			
Duck	128	D (one arrow points left or right)	
Bug	129	B (dark shape-shape with dots-dark shape)	
Crab	130	A (shape type 1-shape type 2-shape type 1)	
Web	131	A (smaller version of same shape in middle)	
(p. 83) *"Find the page where there is a happy face at the bottom."*			
Fork	132	B (shape divided in half)	
Spoon	133	B (center shape different than 2 larger shapes)	
Cup	134	C (same kind of shapes line up horizontally)	
Fish	135	D (triangle in middle)	
(p. 84) *"Find the page where there is a plane at the bottom."*			
Boat	136	D (same kind of larger figure w/ hexagon inside)	
Key	137	C (two identical halves)	
Hat	138	A (similar shape (without corners) divided in half)	
Bug	139	C (parallelogram with small heart and star)	
(p. 85) *"Find the page where there is a cow at the bottom."*			
Train	140	B (4-sided shapes)	
Cup	141	C (2 up arrows, 1 down arrow)	
Chair	142	D (have 2 arrow points)	
Stoplight	143	A (circle is on the corner of the shorter side of the trapezoid)	

Figure Classification Questions Answered Correctly: _____ out of 16

COGAT® QUESTION TYPE 9: PAPER FOLDING (NON-VERBAL SECTION)

Directions for all Paper Folding questions: Look at the top row of pictures. These show a sheet of paper, how it was folded, and how something was cut out of the folded sheet of paper. Look at these pictures that are on the bottom row. Which picture shows how the paper would look after the paper is unfolded?

"Find the row where there is a(n) _____."	Question Number	Answer	Child's Answer
(p. 86) *"Find the page where there is a horse at the bottom."*			
Car	144	D	
Chair	145	B	
Fish	146	B	
(p. 87) *"Find the page where there is a tree at the bottom."*			
Shirt	147	C	
Heart	148	B	
Pencil	149	B	
(p. 88) *"Find the page where there is a stoplight at the bottom."*			
Web	150	C	
Truck	151	A	
Triangle	152	D	
(p. 89) *"Find the page where there is a boat at the bottom."*			
Key	153	A	
Train	154	A	
Cup	155	B	

Paper Folding Questions Answered Correctly: _____ out of 12

Did your child finish the exercises? Here's a certificate for your child! (Please cut along the dotted lines.)

Great Work!

Congratulations to: